The Pilbara OUTBACK AUSTRALIA'S KALEIDOSCOPE OF COLOUR

"Exploration [...] achieve som[...] process of lea[...] surroundings [...] ourselves to find out more about the world and our place in it is as relevant now as ever. Humanity relies on adventurous souls taking risks to progress: it's the human spirit of adventure that lies at the heart of artistic expression, advances in science, medicine, politics or any other sphere...We should not lose this desire to explore nor demean those who seek it, be it the adventure of personal discovery or a more literal journey..."[1]

"Refreshed or depressed? After a week in town it depends a lot on how a person has behaved himself whilst there. However, I do know where my heart lies and am always glad to be on the dusty open road again, loaded with stores, water and fuel, headed for the wide open spaces and wilderness areas where the real pleasures of a bushman's life are to be found".[2]

Proudly supported by

FMG

Hugh Brown www.hughbrown.com

Dedication

To Fiona

The Pilbara
Outback Australia's Kaleidoscope of Colour

ISBN

0 9752054 1 2

November 2005

Hugh Brown
PO Box 1918
BROOME WA 6725
Telephone: +61 418 936 517

Design - *TM Typographics*

Print - *Craft Print International*

A Note from the Author

Midway through 2005, I undertook a bushcraft course conducted by Bob Cooper. While I have spent a lot of time in the bush, the course offered a wealth of information with the potential to one day save one's life. I would strongly commend Bob's courses to anyone travelling into remote Australia. Bob can be contacted at www.bobcoopersurvival.com and conducts regular survival training for the Texas Parks and Wildlife Service. He has also conducted training for the NASA space shuttle crew. And, while on survival, thanks to the management and staff at Nanutarra Roadhouse, on the North-West Coastal Highway, who do the best scones, jam and cream in the Pilbara.

While every effort has been made to ensure its accuracy, the information contained in this book has been included as a guide only and not as a basis for the making of decisions that will vary according to individual needs. Weather and road conditions can change suddenly and people should make their own checks prior to travelling into what are, in many cases, remote areas. People should ensure they have an adequate supply of food, water and spare tyres to sustain them for a considerable period in the event of mechanical breakdown. They should always tell someone where they are going and when they are due back.

Throughout the text, I have frequently used the word "discovered". This is not intended to diminish recognition for the prior inhabitation of Aboriginal peoples. Rather, it merely refers to the identification and naming of the places traversed by early European explorers.

Table of Contents

Acknowledgements

This book is the result of seven years of living, travelling, enjoying and suffering throughout the Pilbara. Many of these photographs would not have been possible without the encouragement and assistance of the following people:

1. To Dennis O'Meara and Paul Rushton for their kind words;

2. To my girlfriend, Fiona who, tirelessly, helped with proofing, choosing photographs and cooking the most beautiful dinners imaginable;

3. To Trevor and Michelle Brodie of Trevelle Engineering who were always willing to assist, throughout the entire project, regardless of whether that involved a two hundred kilometre tow from Marble Bar to Port Hedland, or the ready offer of a bed for the night. They are among the most obliging people that I have met (though we did have to fight at times over the apple-pie);

4. To Ali Spencer for her efforts in proofing the text. She went way beyond what was expected;

5. To the people, characters and companies in, and outside of, the Pilbara who provided so much help in so many ways, including: Rob Bogle, Paul Brady, "Brian" and the "Weather Ferret" at the Bureau of Meteorology, Bob Cooper, Lindsay Copeman, Trevor Corrigal, Alex Dorrington, Ken Duncan, Joe and Maria Farulyas, Craig Faulkner and Wendy Bebbington, Kim Epton, Graham Gardner, Doug Gibson, Mario Hartmann, Julie Heath, Vic Justice, Ray and Murray Kennedy, Lenny Lever, Pat Longland (Roebourne Visitor Centre), Brett and Kelly McRum, Jayne Mayes, Craig and Tammy Mertens, Newcrest Mining Ltd, Damon O'Meara, Noel Parkin, Shane Peters, Pilbara Iron, Philip Quirk, Sipa Resources International NL, Danielle Stefani, Bob Taylor, "Wacka", Ken Walker, "Werner", and Christine Willis;

6. To the staff at the MG Kailis Group for their continued support. It is rare to find such an ethical and committed group of people.

7. To Brian Smallwood and the team at ARB 4 x 4 Accessories in Perth who continue to be strong and encouraging supporters;

8. To John and Peter Robinson and the Bradshaw Foundation (www.bradshawfoundation.com) who have been such great supporters;

9. To Morgan and Nina Neilsen for their generosity. Also, to the people of Fitzroy Crossing who have given their support at various times and added so much colour to my three years there: Terry Babbington, Ian Dickins, Dave Fielder, Ronnie George, Mike Harvey and Helen Devitt, Ken and Sue McLeod, Mad Mick, Rose, Smithy, Stretch, Bruce and Cathy Thorpe, Tony Twidale, Sharon Walsh and all the others (who know who they are);

10. To Greg Taylor at TM Typographics who put in so many hours of his time to make this project what it has now become. His design skills and knowledge of the printing industry have proven absolutely first rate. He can be contacted on telephone 08 9474 2610;

11. To Romeo Marcos and the people at Craft Print (0439 963 397) who have printed this, and my last, book and who have been so easy to deal with. Their reliability, quality and service have been fantastic throughout all of my dealings with them;

12. To Norwest Airwork Aerial Tours at Exmouth and Coral Bay and to Brent Smoothy of Smoothy Helicopters in Newman;

13. To my corporate backers, who saw enough in the project to commit their funds;

14. To Rob and Cath Davies at Pannawonica, Barry Woodward and "Philo" Hathaway at Paraburdoo, and to Bill Aspinall, Graeme Marskell and Grant Carroll at Tom Price;

15. To Dr Martin Van Kranendonk who provided enormous help on assisting me to understand the geology of the Pilbara. Other invaluable help on geological questions was provided by Dr Craig Rugless, Sean O'Connor, Tony Standish and David Pearcey; and,

16. To CALM Karratha, thank you for allowing me access to your excellent library. Similarly, thank you to staff at the Exmouth, Karratha, Marble Bar, Newman, Pannawonica, Paraburdoo, Nullagine, Roebourne, South Hedland and Tom Price libraries.

Foreword

Denis O'Meara

In March 1959 as a 21 year old, I drove the thousand miles from Perth to Marble Bar in a privately built sports car without a hood. I was two days on the (gravel) road between Meekatharra (the halfway point) and Marble Bar without seeing another vehicle going either way. A three-month-old golden Labrador, Baron, was my only companion (who knows, he may have been the great great grandfather of "Kanch"). The 50°C dust, flying stones, engine knocks and constant drinking of warm water were beginning to wear us both down, when, in the late afternoon of the second day, we drove past the first flat top hills north of Roy Hill Station. This was my first recognition that the Pilbara region of Western Australia is unique to the world. My life changed that evening as we made our way to Nullagine, prior to limping into Marble Bar the next day.

A generation later, the wonderful talent of Hugh Brown is introducing this part of the world to many because this dedicated young man has adopted the North-West of Australia as his spiritual home. The craft of photography becomes art in the eyes of those like Hugh, who know that you can spend days and weeks of travail and hard yakka to gain the scene that imprints on minds, globally. When travelling in the remote areas of Australia, a brief vision - light, dust-storm, rain-shower, shadow - can cause the vehicle brakes to go on, because, in that instant, Hugh sees what escapes most of us - an image that will provide a lifetime of pleasure to many and a desire to be there.

A mutual friend in Broome introduced Hugh to me and my son Damon several years ago. We have been privileged to observe the advancement of his career. Several of his photographs grace our offices and homes. As a prospector, I am aware of much of what Hugh has to endure to complete his work. It is not a walk in the park, but thankfully he brings home images of stunning beauty that enhance our lives.

Publication of *The Kimberley: Australia's Wild Outback Wilderness*, was a world-class addition to pictorial Australiana.

The *Pilbara: Outback Australia's Kaleidoscope of Colour*, ranks with all his previous efforts and we are excited by its launch into our world.

DENIS O'MEARA

Paul Rushton

Hugh Brown, "Driving Instructor". These were the words on Hugh's first business cards. It was 1991 and Hugh had just purchased his first 4WD, a Subaru wagon. Not long after he purchased the vehicle, Hugh decided to go on a camping, fishing and photography trip to the Victorian High Country with a friend. He was living in Geelong at the time and planned to spend his time near Craig's Hut before heading into the King River catchment area. Three days into the trip, I received a phone call. Just prior to descending a hazardous 4WD track, one essentially comprised of washouts and granite boulders, Hugh stepped out of the vehicle to photograph the track they were about to descend. He heard a noise. Suddenly, his new 4WD had dislodged from gear and took off down the hill. As it gathered speed, it rolled over and onto its roof. Hugh was devastated.

After the initial shock had subsided, Hugh and his mate set to "righting" the vehicle. Out came a chainsaw and saplings were pushed under the roof to act as rollers. The vehicle was dragged down the hill and then, using a large branch as leverage, tipped onto its side. Hugh saw a great photo opportunity. He had his mate take a series of photos of himself standing next to the vehicle as it stood on its side. They then proceeded to start the vehicle up and drove it 200 kilometres home in darkness and thick fog. It was teaming with rain and the vehicle, by now, had a caved-in roof and was missing a windscreen. When he got home he had some cards printed using one of these photos.

Hugh's passion for adventure and excitement has always been a part of him. When he moved to Western Australia toward the end of 1998, it was with sense of a trepidation. The vastness, the isolation, the culture, the people and the incredible geography of the region provided Hugh with a great test. To be true to himself, Hugh could only live in one way...to the extreme. Hugh's passion for photography took over his life and, coupled with his thirst for adventure, Hugh began to produce some extraordinary photos.

The extreme side of Hugh has enabled him to go where most people do not go. In photographing these images Hugh has fallen from cliffs, spent days bogged in mud to his vehicle's axles and endured weeks in the outback without seeing other people. Hugh has simply lived life to the full, but, throughout, has retained his fantastic sense of humour and his likeable nature.

There are many stories I could tell about Hugh. But more importantly, Hugh has been a great friend to me, and many, many, others. He is a person with enormous capability. He is a caring and compassionate person. He is a person with a great sense of humour and intellect. He is adventurous, resilient and driven. Hugh has drawn on all of these talents to produce this book. I am fortunate to know Hugh well. I can identify the person, the passion and the adventure in this book. For those who have not been as fortunate to know Hugh, simply enjoy the book for what it is: stunning.

PAUL RUSHTON

Introduction

Life in the north is never dull. As I write this piece, the countryside is a swirling mass of dust, horizontal rain and some of the most dramatic and electrifying fork lightning imaginable. I sit in a hotel room pondering my next couple of days and the possibility of an expensive 200 kilometre tow from Marble Bar to Port Hedland. A lightning strike to my vehicle at 60 kilometres an hour put paid to that and the welfare of my A\$3,000 HF[3] radio and the electrics in my vehicle. And the Canning Stock Route saw to the well-being of my front right shock absorber, UHF[4] aerial and long range AM/FM antenna. The Pilbara in the height of summer is at its harshest. Temperatures throughout the course of this trip, which has primarily been in, and to the far east of, Marble Bar, have been in the mid to high forties. Marble Bar recorded a 48^{0}C last week. But all of this notwithstanding, I would not want to be anywhere else. The Pilbara, like the Kimberley to the north, is at its most spectacular when at its least forgiving.

Compilation of this book proved to be far more challenging than was the case with my 2004 book - *The Kimberley: Australia's Wild Outback Wilderness* - perhaps far more challenging than I would have liked. Many of the photographs for this book were shot during the height of one of the hottest summers in many years: it was important to me that I show the Pilbara across its many seasons and moods. Marble Bar had recorded over 100 consecutive days where the mercury exceeded the old hundred mark and January 2005 saw Marble Bar record an average daily maximum of 44.6^{0}C; its hottest on record. In March,

two ill-equipped travellers perished through dehydration and heatstroke on the perimeters of the Great and Little Sandy Deserts. The January lightning strike preceded another frighteningly close call three weeks later when a huge bolt hammered the road right next to my vehicle as I drove into Nullagine. It was only a fortuitous five-inch dump of rain in mid-July of 2005 that rejuvenated the Pilbara. Some of these photos reflect the region's 'rebirth' from the depression of what had been a most severe drought.

Despite the challenges, my love for the Pilbara continues unabated. Photography, for me, is as much about the adventure (the risks to put it bluntly) that one confronts often out here, as it is about the art and science of making a photograph. I wouldn't want photography without the adventure, or adventure without the photography. In many ways, I prefer the country at its harshest: when 65^{0}C surface temperatures melt the glues holding the soles of one's shoes from their leather uppers (as proved to be the case with my A\$400 hiking boots); or when rain renders rocks so slippery, and gorges so treacherous, that being in the wrong place at the wrong moment can easily prove fatal. As a photographer, I like the motif that 'the best time to photograph a place is when it is supposed to be the worst time to be there'. At least that way, I know that there is a good chance that I will come away with something different.

Here, I was in Weano Gorge in Karijini National Park during light rain. One should always exit the Karijini gorges if it is raining or threatening to rain. Flash-flooding is a real danger and has claimed numerous lives. On this occasion, the rise in water levels was noticeable as I beat a hasty retreat.

"Pilbara" thought to be an Aboriginal name denoting one of "dry or dried-out" or fish (mullet);

Pilbara incorporates the Town of Port Hedland and the Shires of Ashburton, East Pilbara and Roebourne. For this book, the Shire of Exmouth has been included to form the "Greater Pilbara"; and,

Greater Pilbara covers an area of 518,520 square kilometres and has 40,000 – 45,000 inhabitants.

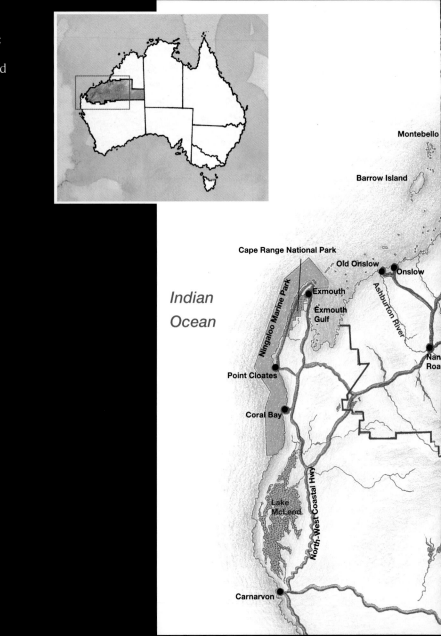

Montebello

Barrow Island

Cape Range National Park

Old Onslow

Onslow

Indian
Ocean

Ningaloo Marine Park

Exmouth

Exmouth
Gulf

Ashburton River

Point Cloates

Nan
Roa

Coral Bay

Lake
McLeod

North-West Coastal Hwy

Carnarvon

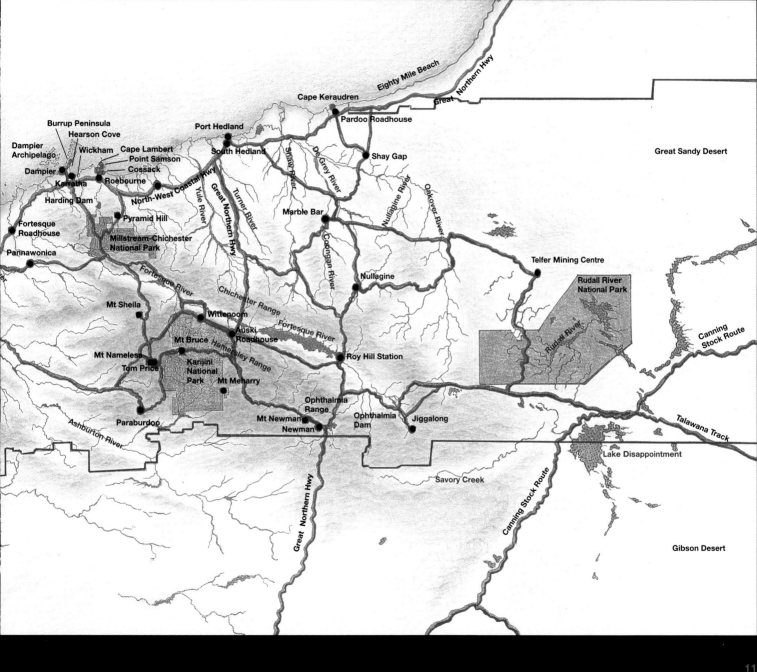

Port Hedland and Surrounds

Port Hedland is located on a tidal inlet 1,600 kilometres north of Perth. The inlet was discovered in April, 1863 by Captain Peter Hedland, while on board the vessel, *Mystery*. He was seeking to locate a suitable landing spot (that was also near to fresh-water) from which pioneer pastoralist, Walter Padbury, could unload his soon-to-follow first stock shipment. Hedland named the inlet Mangrove Harbour, though the name was changed to its current name by a government navigator, Hunt, some two months after the original sighting.[5]

Known to local Aboriginal tribes as Marrapikurrinya, after three reliable freshwater soaks that existed in the area, Port Hedland was gazetted as a town on 22 October, 1896. It was established to service the east Pilbara goldfields around Marble Bar and Nullagine. The port of Cossack was considered to be too distant for the Nullagine and Marble Bar fields. Port Hedland benefited from not being at the mouth of a major river-system which meant that it did not silt up to the same extent as ports such as Cossack. This enabled it to take larger ships. Prior to that time, it existed as a series of buildings that serviced surrounding pastoral properties and the generally associated pearling industry.[6]

It was not until the 29th of March, 1961 that the foundations for Port Hedland's stunning future growth were laid. Prior to the Second World War, Commonwealth and State laws had been enacted that prevented the exportation of iron ore and disallowed discoverers from obtaining security of tenure over their finds. This was intended to serve two aims. Australia

Aerial Photograph of Port Hedland

The longest ship to have docked in Port Hedland was the 328.6 metre *Hyundai Giant*. Loaded with 234,544 tonnes of iron ore bound for Korea, this was also the largest single cargo to have left the port.[11] With iron ore demand booming on the back of insatiable demand from China, records are falling monthly and this trend looks set to continue into the foreseeable future.

did not wish for its iron to come back as bullets and bombs. It also did not wish to stimulate undue foreign interest, and hence heighten the risk of invasion, by stating the true magnitude of its iron reserves.[7]

Today Port Hedland is a town predicated very much on the region's massive iron ore industry. In the year ended 30 June, 2005, some 108 million tonnes of iron ore, salt and bulk minerals were processed through its port, making it Australia's largest export port and the world's third largest.[8] BHP-Billiton plans to increase its iron ore output to around 150 million tonnes over the next five years and there is scope for a further 20 ship births to be added to the existing five.[9] A typical ore carrier is around 300 metres long, carries 200,000 tonnes of ore and is loaded at the rate of 10,000 tonnes an hour (making for a turnaround of just over 24 hours).[10] When one ship is loaded there is another ready to take its place. It is astonishing to witness the sheer volume and size of ships that pass through the port.

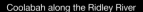

Coolabah along the Ridley River

Located near one of Atlas Gold's tenements, in the vicinity of Port Hedland, this was another beautiful location that I would never have thought existed so close to a major population centre. Atlas had been taking clay samples from the beds of surrounding watercourses with a view to testing the level of gold mineralisation. Because clay absorbs gold from groundwater, it is seen to be a more thorough indicator of gold mineralisation than conventional gravel-sampling, which picks up alluvial nuggets only.[12]

Drill Samples - Ord Range

Contract geologist, Tony Standish, displays iron ore
sample trays at one of Atlas Gold's tenements in the
vicinity of Port Hedland. Drill samples are taken at
various depths, stored in trays of the nature seen here
(with the depth marked), and analysed on site. They are
then sent away for further testing by metallurgists.

Unnamed Rock-Hole in the Ord Range

This waterhole is located in a range that I had driven past many times, without even thinking that it could contain something so beautiful. The rock seen in the foreground is part of a broader, banded iron formation that extends as far south as Whim Creek. In places, it is up to one kilometre thick.

DOM's Hill

This hill was named after local identity and prospector, Denis O'Meara, around 1987, by the exploration manager at Maralga Mining. Denis was the first person to find gold there.[13] The geology of this peak is incredibly complex. It is thought that a chert band (chert is very hard and comprised predominantly of silica) was deposited in shallow seas in a period of volcanic activity some 2.5 billion years ago. Then, during a period of tectonic activity, a layer of ultra-mafic rock (ie, nickel bearing) was thrust up at an angle over the chert layer. Over time this eroded leaving the harder chert band exposed. It is thought that a solution of silica was then forced up through a fault and eventually crystallised into a quartz cap that overlays the chert. A truly stunning location.[14]

Cape Keraudren and the Eighty Mile Beach[15]

Commencing at Cape Keraudren, some 110 kilometres north of Port Hedland, and extending for 220 kilometres north to Cape Missiessy, Eighty Mile Beach is around 100 metres wide and incorporates a number of muddy embayments. The first steps in its creation are thought to have occurred when the sea breached alluvial coastal plains and sediment was progressively deposited in intertidal waters. These are now evident as shallow marine muds which spread across the plains. As the sea retreated, equivalent sedimentary environments migrated seaward also. Grass covered the supra-tidal flats as they became inactive and a series of up to four parallel beach ridges developed along Eighty Mile Beach.

Where active dune building is occurring, there are typically four dunes: an incipient fore-dune, an established fore-dune, a swale and a hind-dune. The appearance of these four beach ridges suggests that sea levels have fluctuated markedly over time. A dune is initially formed as an incipient fore-dune that then matures with the deposition of further sand and the encroachment of vegetation. However, both this and the incipient fore-dune are dynamic environments given their exposure to high wind action at certain times of the year. This is particularly the case during cyclone season when the incipient fore-dune may be removed totally and the established fore-dune severely scoured. The coastal floodplain is typically subjected to flooding through cyclone events once every five years.

Cape Keraudren appears to have first been sighted by two French ships on 2 April, 1803 as part of the 1801 - 1803 French voyages of discovery under the command of Nicholas Baudin. Baudin was captain of the *Geographe* and Louis-Claude de Freycinet, captain of the *Casuarina*. Though it was certainly seen by both ships on this day, the name Cape Keraudren was not recorded in Baudin's journal. As Baudin died in September 1803, it was left to Freycinet to publish maps of the expedition and it was his 1824 published chart (Carte - De La Terre De Witt) that first showed the Cap Keraudren name; a name that was changed to Cape Keraudren in 1905. I was not able to determine therefore whether it was Freycinet or Baudin who named the Cape, though it was most likely named after Pierre Francois Keraudren (1769 - 1857), physician in charge of medical services at Brest and author of works on diseases of seamen.[16]

Marble Bar and Marble Bar Pool

Marble Bar owes its foundation to the discovery of gold at Prospector's Gully in 1891 by Ted Francis, Harry Jenkins and Jim Edmonstone, although it was not officially gazetted as a town until 13 July, 1893. Now home to approximately 350 people, the town is estimated to have been home to 500 to 750 Europeans during the peak of the gold rush. Late in 1942, construction of an airstrip was completed on an iron ridge at nearby Corruna Downs Station and this was used as a launch pad for bombing raids on Surabaya and Denpasar in Indonesia. Though they tried on many occasions, the Japanese never succeeded in locating it.

Marble Bar, and the Pilbara more generally, is also home to the oldest geology on earth. The Pilbara Craton (as it is geologically known) is an unusually thick piece of buoyant crust that could not be recycled to the earth's mantle as was the fate with most of the crust on early earth. Numerous episodes of basaltic volcanism left the residual underlying mantle cold and dense and without melt-producing elements that would have seen the crust recycled: a "lithosperic root". It is by virtue of this "lithosperic root" that the Pilbara Craton survives today: like a big carrot extending 400 kilometres into the mantle and floating around on the earth's surface like a bobbing cork or iceberg.

In 2001, the oldest dated rock on earth was discovered on Warrawagine Station: to the north-east of Marble Bar. Measuring only $1m^3$ in size, the rock is a tightly folded gneissic tonalite (a type of granite that has been metamorphosed through volcanic heat) that has been dated at around 3.65 billion years.[17] Stromatolites found at Chinaman's Creek, also near Marble Bar, are the world's oldest. These are dome-shaped formations, contained within rock, and incorporate intricate textures that many believe to have been created by colonies of microbes that could represent the beginnings of life on earth. They are thought to have been deposited in a shallow lagoon or river-mouth which might have offered a home for early life.[18]

Locals and visitors play "two-up" at the annual Marble Bar race-day: about 8 kilometres from the Marble Bar Travellers' Stop (08 9176 1166): one of the town's premier accommodation facilities and eateries. Marble Bar takes its name from the jasper bar at nearby Marble Bar Pool on the Coongan River. The jasper bar was discovered and named by pioneer pastoralist, Nathaniel Cooke, during the 1880s, and he erroneously thought it to be comprised of marble. The nearby Comet Gold Mine was discovered in late 1935 by local resident, Tommy Starr. It turned out to be one of the richest mines in the Pilbara and was originally called Halley's Comet Mine "because a mine of such quality is found only once in a lifetime". It once had the tallest smoke-stack (75m) in the southern hemisphere.[19]

Marble Bar Pool - Coongan River

Marble is a metamorphosed limestone, the limestone of
which has been precipitated chemically from seawater:
usually, by living organisms. The limestone has crystallised
when the water has become supersaturated, or, when it has
been transformed by organisms into shells or skeletons.
Jasper is an iron-bearing silica rock, constituted usually by
around 99% silica and a dusting of haematite (the oxidised
form of iron). Haematite gives the jasper its characteristic
red colour. Jasper is formed by the chemical precipitation of
silica and iron from seawater (again when the water
becomes supersaturated).[20]

Pilbara Weather and Dust Storm near Marble Bar

A dust storm is essentially a large wall of dust that builds up at the leading edge of a desert thunderstorm. At the heart of a thunderstorm is a rising updraft of warm air and a falling downdraft of cold air. As the falling, cooling, air hits the ground, it spreads out - away from the storm centre - creating a gust front of wind. This can be very fast and, in the case of a dust storm, dust and sand are lifted in its wake to create a dark, towering, cloud of dust.[21]

Marble Bar is today promoted as being Australia's hottest town. However, the State's highest recorded temperature, 50.5°C, was in fact achieved at another Pilbara station, Mardie (near Dampier), on 19 February, 1998. Marble Bar achieved infamy for its 160 consecutive days where the mercury exceeded 37.8°C (100°F in the old scale) between 31 October, 1923 and 7 April, 1924. The Pilbara's lowest recorded maximum was 10.6°C at Nullagine on 11 August, 1972. The highest recorded minimum temperature was 35.5°C at Wittenoom on 21 January, 1973 and the lowest recorded minimum temperature was -2.2°C at Nullagine on 20 July, 1965. The State's highest recorded rainfall in a 24 hour period was 747mm at Whim Creek, also a Pilbara station, on 3 April, 1898 and the Pilbara's highest recorded monthly rainfall was 929mm at Whim Creek in April of the same year.[22]

This dust storm precéded my vehicle being struck by lightning by about 15 or 20 minutes (I was driving when struck). Having taken shots of the granite seen in the foreground, I decided to sit back and wait for a sunset that offered some promise. In the distance, I noticed a small cloud of dust and initially thought it to be that of a road train travelling en route to Nullagine. However, the cloud grew, and I soon realised that I was in fact witnessing something far more spectacular. I raced for my camera and continued to shoot as it passed directly overhead.

Lenny Lever - Lever's Store - Marble Bar

Though he considers himself not to be a local - "I've only been here 35 years" - Lenny Lever is another of the characters in Australia's north who have had both an interesting past and made a significant contribution. In years to come he will be remembered as a bull-dozer driver, prospector, miner, shop-keeper, mechanic, powerhouse operator, airport operator, Watercorp worker and State Battery driver (with many of these tasks being undertaken concurrently). Perhaps more significantly, he will also be remembered as the driving force behind a wall in the Marble Bar main street that commemorates the lives and hardships suffered by those that opened up the Pilbara: from Whim Creek to the Northern Territory border and up to the Eighty Mile Beach. He noted to me in February, 2005:

"I went over to the Shire to pay a bill one day and a tourist brought in a homemade tombstone. I think the bastard pinched it off a grave myself and later $%^& himself. He said he got it off a windrow of dirt out at North Pole [a mining province]. I'd been knocking around out there for about two and a half years and knew of four graves. But then I thought that if he did in fact find it on a windrow then maybe I had bull-dozed it? That kicked me off. So I wondered how many more there were around here. The girl in the Shire got me a book. A girl workin' here was doin' it and I was doin' it. Got another 20 names to go on it now. And I'd say they'll keep turning up. There's a 198 of the bastards. When I finish I might go and see if I can find a few more graves...."

"No matter where you go, you see memorials of soldiers. There's none for the pioneers. Them pioneers would have suffered up just as much as some of the soldiers did. You imagine pushin' a wheel-barrow through some of the country from Roebourne to here. They didn't know where they were goin' either. No roads, no maps. And that's why you see so many graves out there. They died like flies: adults, kids. There's no recognition anywhere in Australia. So I built one in Marble Bar....It doesn't have any of those that are buried in a cemetery."

Lenny proved to be a veritable mine of information in relation to the history of the Marble Bar and Nullagine areas: particularly the stories of the pioneering days. He referred to the case of a street party that started when two wagon drivers bumped into one another in the middle of Marble Bar:

"There was one wagon comin' [from Port Hedland] loaded full of alcohol. One goin' out. They hadn't seen one another for a while. Decided to drink one bottle. Ended up bein' a big party and they drank the whole wagon. Station workers, prospectors, the whole town. 'Won't miss one bottle will they?' One bottle went to two bottles, three bottles, four bottles. Some poor pub was waitin' for his tucker and a store waitin' for his supplies. That history's gone. We've got motor car now. If we can't get to Port Hedland in two hours we complain. We get a flat tyre, we've had a bastard of a trip."

Lenny attributes the decline of Marble Bar, from the time when he first arrived there, to the closure of the State Battery - "that knocked the prospectors around" - and the closure of the tin mines: "Three stores have gone out of the main street. There's nobody out in the bush anymore. There was a store out at the Brockman River, there was three tin mines employing a hundred black fellas. Three tin mines out the Hillside way employing same amount of black fellas. They're all gone."

One Mile Gorge

I first visited One Mile Gorge in 1999. At the time, I was driving an old beat-up Subaru wagon that struggled to negotiate creek crossings and the like. It had achieved the "distinction" of some 16 punctures in the six months that I had been in the north. My diary of the time notes:

"I headed into the scrub along a very rough four wheel drive track with a degree of trepidation. I was getting into remote and unforgiving country, but I figured that I had twenty litres of water and a camera. What more could I ask for! Six kilometres in, I had to do a 360^0 turn on the side of a hill and at that point the car packed up. Rather than panic, I determined that I should first check the gorge out and then work out how the hell I was going to get out of here. Went for a walk, but could not find the gorge, so started a walk for the main road with my camera (figuring that you never know when you might need to take a photo)...

[A]mazingly, the local pastoralist had decided to make a trip out here. He picked me up and the two of us pulled part of the carby apart, cleaned it, and cleaned the oil filter, and abra cadabra, the car started up...The gorge turned out to be magic. Beautiful, orange, red and white cliffs, and some nice pools and chasms. Worth coming back for a photo.....The only problem was that before the gorge I achieved another puncture. Now up to 16 and by now I had used my two spares. Prayed for bitumen and to get there fast as I still had some very very rough and sharp stones to cross. Plus changing the tyre was hard as there were bull ants everywhere...Ouch!"

Doolena Gorge

Located on the Coongan River to the north of Marble Bar, the name Doolena Gap first appeared in the field-book of E.W. Geyer in 1962. It can be quite a nice spot when seen at the right time of the day.[23]

Glen Herring Gorge

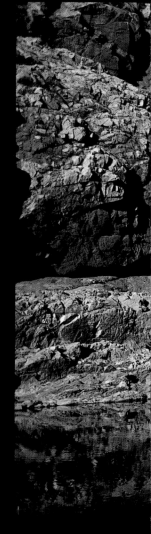

Glen Herring Gorge is one of the more beautiful and readily accessible gorges around Marble Bar. The creek would appear to have taken its name from Glen Herring Pool; so named by Francis Gregory on 20 August, 1861. His diary notes:

"After a few hours' scramble...we came upon a small stream trending east, containing several springs, surrounded by high grass and flags, gradually leading us by sunset into a deep pass, walled in by cliffs and bluffs from 100 to 300 feet high; the stream having joined several larger ones from the southward, now occupying nearly the whole width of the valley. We encamped in one of the wildest and most romantic-looking spots to be found in this part of Australia, to which we gave the name of Glen Herring, from a fish bearing a resemblance to a herring being found in the stream."[24]

Long-time Marble Bar local, Alex Dorrington, noted in discussions I had with him that one of Glen Herring's waterholes had a deep shaft. "When we were younger we tried to drop some weights down to test its depth but couldn't reach the bottom."

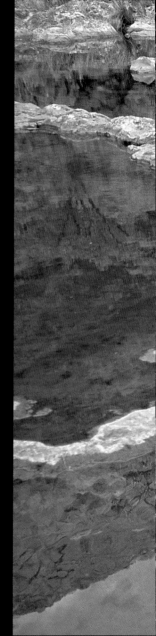

Evening Reflections: Glen Herring Gorge

Carawine Pool

Carawine Pool is located on the Oakover River, about 140 kilometres to the east-south-east of Marble Bar. On my return in January, 2005 (the mercury reached 47°C the day I was there!), I was interested to see the changes since my trip some two years earlier. In March 2004, Cyclone Fay shed nearly 400 millimetres of rain in a 24 hour period upstream near the Nifty copper mine. Severe flash-flooding washed away many of the tall shelter-giving paperbarks and river-gums that had stood for generations. Despite what I had heard, I was pleased to see that it has retained much of its original beauty.

The section of the Oakover River incorporating Carawine Gorge, Upper Carawine Gorge and Carawine Pool was first traversed by Francis Gregory on the 30th August, 1861 during his expedition to explore the "north-west as a preliminary to actual settlement". His journal noted: "we therefore followed the river up for seven or eight miles, through fine open forest country, and encamped near a deep pool, in which were caught 10 or 12 dozen small trout, which, with cockatoos and ducks, afforded an important addition to our ration of only seven ounces of meat. This river was named the Oakover".[25]

Carawine Pool averages around seven metres in depth. The 90 metre cliff on the pool's western bank has been created where the Oakover River (thought to be at least 250 million years old) has carved through hard, reddish-grey, Carawine Dolomite rock during flood times. This, over time, has weathered to a brown surface. While the pool offers good swimming, care should be taken. Thick reeds along part of the river can be treacherous and are said to have resulted in a number of drownings.[26]

Running Waters (Eel Pool)

Running Waters is located on the Oakover River, upstream of Carawine Gorge. Nearby Skull Springs (so named after an Aboriginal skull was found there in 1886), located on the Davis River, a tributary of the Oakover, was perhaps the birthplace of one of the most important Australian Aboriginal rights movements when a major meeting was held there in 1942. At this meeting spoke white miner and prospector Don McLeod who, like a number of senior Aboriginal people, had become concerned that the wages of Aboriginal station hands did not equate to those of their white counterparts. This was largely a function of the labour shortage brought about by the Second World War. Pastoralists had agreed to "look after" all station Aborigines in return for Government pegging wages and preventing the station Aborigines from moving into the towns.[27]

The upshot of the Skull Springs meeting was that, on 1 May, 1946, some 800 Aboriginal station workers walked off 20 stations throughout the Pilbara. The date was chosen by McLeod and his followers to coincide with the end of the war, International Labour Day and the beginning of the shearing season. The strikers had not wished to disrupt the supply of wool during the war and the shearing season was the busiest time of year. The strike lasted until 1949, when suitable wages and conditions were negotiated at Mt Edgar and Limestone stations. On the basis of these negotiations, and over the next 12 months, other Pilbara stations adopted similar new working conditions. Many strikers never returned to the stations, choosing instead to stay in their own self-managed communities; Jiggalong and Yandeyarra being some of the more prominent examples.[28]

Whether or not McLeod's actions were beneficial in the long-term is a question that will always remain open for debate. On the one hand, his actions no doubt led to an improvement in the wages and conditions of those workers whose relative lack of education in the white man world opened them up to exploitation by the unscrupulous. However, there were those pastoralists who did do the right thing by their Aboriginal employees. What must be remembered is that employment of Aboriginal station workers came with the inherent obligation to feed, clothe and shelter their many associated family members, many of whom did not contribute to the efficient workings of the stations. The departure of these people from the stations, the majority of whom chose not to return, led to a loosening of their ties with their traditional lands. Other 'evils' such as drugs and alcohol were also more readily available in towns and self-managed communities. Over time these have loosened the control of the old people over the young. What was once a vibrant and strong culture is now a shadow of its former self.

Cameleer, H.M. Barker, who used to cut Running Waters' giant cadgabutts for building purposes described it thus: "...there is a wonderful place on the Oakover River called Running Waters, a fine big spring gushing out of a limestone bank and forming a waterhole a quarter of a mile long and then running on a few miles until it loses itself in the sand. Quite permanent, and perfect drinking water, it is the only spring of its sort in the north-west barring the Millstream on the Tableland. I know both places, but Running Waters is the more beautiful. The big waterhole is surrounded by giant cadgabutt trees, very straight, a kind of fern-leafed tree with red and white flowers that must be Indigenous to the place as I have seen it nowhere else."[29]

Rudall River National Park and the Canning Stock Route

I first travelled to Rudall River National Park in August, 2002 during a solo trip from Victoria's south-west to Broome, via the Gibson Desert. It had long held an interest for me, if for no other reason than it might reasonably hold claim to being Australia's most remote National Park. On top of that, it is probably one of Australia's least photographed National Parks. The experience certainly matched my anticipation. Rudall River offers a combination of rugged sandstone ranges, cooling intermittent waterholes teaming with animal and bird life, and rich red desert-scape.

Rudall River National Park was created in 1977 and is located at the perimeters of the Great Sandy and Little Sandy Deserts. Known to its Aboriginal traditional custodians as Karlamilyi[30], Rudall River was named by explorer and prospector Frank Hann, somewhere between 5 April and 10 April 1897.[31] At 1,283,706 hectares it is Western Australia's largest National Park, Australia's second largest and more than two and a half times larger than the Grand Canyon National Park in Arizona.[32] Near the northern boundary of the park lies the Kintyre uranium deposit and, to date, reserves of at least 36,000 tonnes of uranium oxide have been identified.[33] Any mining at this location will raise difficult environmental and political challenges.

Evening Light - Tjingkulatjajarra Pool - Rudall River

The Rudall River flows, as a general rule, during two out of every three years: typically after cyclonic rains have pushed a long way inland from the coast. Rainfall averages around 200mm annually; significantly less than the 4400mm lost to evaporation each year. In between these times it dries up into a series of long deep pools, lined with rivergums and a diverse array of bird life.[41] As I write this, I sit on the banks of the river itself. It is mid January, and the temperature is nudging 45⁰C. That notwithstanding, the feeling of isolation, the refreshment of a cooling swim and the voices of the many birds make the experience of being out here quite wonderful.

Charles Wells and George Jones were probably the first Europeans to enter the area now incorporated within Rudall River National Park when they branched off from the Calvert Expedition to explore and map country to the west. Cut off by salt lakes, they returned to Separation Well, before heading north to try and find the main expedition. They died of thirst before they could locate Joanna Spring. Lawrence Wells, the expedition's leader, reprovisioned at Noonkanbah Station (near Fitzroy Crossing) and was later to make four attempts to find the lost men. William Frederick Rudall, after whom the Park takes its name, set off from Roebourne to join the search and made three attempts. It was during this search that he discovered the Rudall River.[34]

Rudall River National Park is perhaps the only park in Australia where the combined number of its reptile and frog species (at least 52 and 7) nearly equals that of its bird species (72).[35] Most mammals larger than the spinifex hopping mouse have disappeared: mainly as a result of exposure to high density feral fox and cat populations. These mammals include the black-footed rock wallaby, the possum and the boodie.[36] In 1998, teachers from the nearby Punmu Aboriginal Community captured an Australian Marsupial Mole: a rare and endangered small and blind mammal with no ears and eyes. It was the first to be captured and was immediately transported to a new home in Perth to enable future study by zoologists.[37]

August Reflections - Desert Queen Baths

A quite stunning series of rock pools in the Broadhurst Range in the eastern portion of Rudall River National Park. The pools were named by independent prospector, Jean-Paul Turcaud in 1970 after the beauty and seclusion of the pools put him in mind of a poem about a place "where the queen of the desert comes to bathe".[40]

Rivergums in a Tributary of the Rudall River

A key feature of Rudall River is the number of wild dromedary (single hump) camels that roam within its boundaries: in fact, they are the only wild dromedaries found anywhere throughout the world.[38] The first camels are thought to have been released into Western Australia in the early 1870s by one or more of the Gosse, Warburton and Giles expeditions. Until 1897, when importation was banned due to intense lobbying from operators of traditional horse teams (affected by reduced cartage rates), some 7,000 - 10,000 camels are estimated to have been brought into Western Australia from South Australia and overseas.[39]

Hanging Rock

Hanging Rock was discovered and named by explorer, and leader of the Calvert Search Party, William F. Rudall, on 29 April, 1897.

"...about 1/4 mile west is a peculiar rock on the flat, it has the appearance of having the remainder gradually falling away leaving 2 great boulders about 30ft high standing on a low mound".[42]

Explorer Frank Hann noted, on seeing the rock on 29 April, 1897: "I saw a square rock about fifty feet high straight up. I never saw one like it before".[43]

Hanging Rock is located on the western perimeter of the National Park. My visit there was undertaken alone, and while the drive out was beautiful - particularly the vibrant red of the generally parallel sand dunes - there were some anxious moments in negotiating thick, soft sand in a steep-sided creek.

This time exposure, taken over a period of four hours or more, shows the rotation of the stars around the South Celestial Pole. Due south, the location of which can be determined easily by reference to the Southern Cross and its pointer stars (most good survival books show exactly how), can be identified by drawing a line directly from the South Celestial Pole to the horizon: useful knowledge for navigating at night.

The Canning Stock Route and Beyond (Into the Little Sandy, Great Sandy and Gibson Deserts)

In deciding which areas to incorporate within this book, there were a couple of areas that I felt could not be excluded, primarily because of their beauty and the fact that they fall within the boundaries of the East Pilbara Shire (boundaries which extend right through to the Northern Territory border). As I write this piece, the air is punctuated with the screeches of galahs amidst the red sandstone walls and white rivergum trunks of Durba Gorge, in the Durba Range (to the south of Lake Disappointment). There has not been a soul in sight for some days: perhaps because it is now mid January and I'm probably the only one silly enough to come here at this time of year??? Nevertheless, the Canning is a magical place, whatever the time of year and whatever the time of day.

Sunset on the Canning Stock Route

The deep red sands of the Great Sandy, Little Sandy and Gibson Deserts are essentially quartz grains coated with a film of iron oxide, though chemical tests have thus far failed to establish the source from which they were derived. However, the presence of well-established eucalypts on dune crests suggests a fairly stable surface and that sand movement has at best been superficial.[45]

Constructed over two years (between 1908 and 1910), the Canning Stock Route owes its existence to the ingenuity and bushcraft of Alfred Canning. Hailed at the time as "the last of the explorers", Canning lead a team of 31 people, 70 camels and two horses in the construction of 68 wells, over 1,400 kilometres from Wiluna to Halls Creek. The route was established to enable Kimberley cattle to be sold in southern markets by virtue of the fact that ticks would not survive the harsh desert conditions on the journey south (tick-infested cattle were not permitted to be sold on the open market in Australia).

Seven mobs of cattle, mainly from Billiluna, were driven south from the time of its opening in 1911 until 1917, when dipping was introduced and cattle could then be transported south by boat. In 1922, disease broke out in the Kimberley and the ban was re-imposed. Canning returned from retirement and, in 1930, led a team to re-establish the route; it then being used until 1958.[44] Canning determined, after Well 11, to call the wells by their Aboriginal names where practicable, the purpose being to enable drovers to ask the Aborigines for directions to the wells. Each of Durba, Biella, Diebel and Killagurra are the local place names, though many drovers thought that Durba was in fact Killagurra.

This photograph was captured just south of the Pilbara region; on the Gunbarrel Highway. It was taken in the Gibson Desert and is characteristic of much of the scenery that one enjoys when out on the Talawanna Track and Gary Highway, both of which lie east of the Canning Stock Route. I so love the peace and quiet out there and the fact that you can drive for days without seeing another person.

Nullagine and Surrounds

Nullagine[46]

Nullagine is situated on the Nullagine River, at the exact point at which pioneer pastoralist Nathaniel Cooke crossed during his return from his 1882-3 explorations of the east Pilbara. It owes its foundation to the discovery of payable gold in the Conglomerates by Cooke on 9 June, 1888. Nullagine is an Aboriginal name, though its meaning is not known. It is probable that the Nullagine River was named by Cooke during the late 1880s.

At its peak in 1899, Nullagine was home to some 271 people (270 men and 1 female!). This population increase was driven largely by the British investment boom of 1895; a boom that lead to the establishment of the region's first battery in 1895, and a further two by 1897. In 1895, over 30 British companies were being established each month (eventually reaching a total of 342) to invest in West Australian goldfields. These were driven largely by the realisation that richer deposits could be found at depths previously thought to be uneconomic. In 1899, due to development constraints imposed by a scarcity of water, the government sank wells at Middle Creek, Mosquito Creek, Sandy, Elsie and Cookes Creek. This led to the development of five main areas: the Middle Creek - 20 Mile Creek area, the Mosquito Creek area, the Eastern Creek area, the Elsie area and the Biljim area.

The Nullagine field was situated adjacent to the Nullagine River and a number of other tributaries of the De Grey. It incorporated alluvial deposits of three classes. First, there were alluvium deposits of existing creeks. Second, there were alluvium deposits of older creek beds. And, third, there were old alluvium deposits or deep leads that bore no relationship with existing streams or country configuration. All three types of deposit were rich, though there are no accurate figures available as to the gold that was taken prior to the establishment of the Mines Department.

1902 brought about some considerable interest in diamonds, and, though records of production are vague, sizes, of the 25 ounces known to have been found, ranged from $^1/_{16}$th to 1/2 carrots per diamond. Though no records of diamonds in the area have been reported since these initial discoveries, they did give Nullagine the distinction of being the first place in Australia to have produced saleable diamonds. By 1906, the mines began to decline once again and many miners began to anticipate being able to work more profitably on the construction of a new railway in the district. Others left to work on the new copper and tin mines near Marble Bar. The British Exploration Company, the major company operating in the area, would appear to have been forced into liquidation: perhaps because, like most other British investment companies in WA gold mining, its method of investment and control was geared to promotional and speculative gains in London. As this company was the holder of the largest mining properties in the Nullagine, its liquidation was to have a great effect on production from the Nullagine field.

Today, Nullagine is a town that could be on the precipice of significant expansion. Wedgetail Exploration has purchased the local hotel and plans to commence a gold mining operation at the nearby Dromedaries, while Fortesque Metals plans the establishment of a major iron-ore mine some 70 kilometres to the town's south. Nullagine is a special place, and though it does not look to offer much at first appearance, it contains some of the most interesting people, and is near to some of the most beautiful places, that I have seen and met in my seven years of travelling throughout the Pilbara.

This gorge is located in the vicinity of a large pegmatite dyke. Where this geology is found, tin and other metals such as beryllium, tantalite, mica and feldspar are often found also. My main recollection of capturing this photograph was that the access track was rougher than most that one could be expected to travel in the Pilbara.

Sunset along the Old Anthill Road

Located along the old "Anthill Road", the area around Castle Hill
was once a major mining centre. The Conglomerates (the hills
located immediately behind Nullagine and on the other side of
town to Castle Hill) were thought to have once been a low-lying
point, many millions of years ago, into which ancient creeks and
rivers fed. These creeks and rivers brought a variety of rock
types that later compacted to create the conglomerate geology
that we see today. Over time, the less resistant surrounding
country has eroded, leaving the Conglomerates to stand above

Rivergums - Marble Bar Road

A word of advice for the prospective tourist/ prospector to Nullagine, the locals detest being asked "where's the gold?" As at least half a dozen commented to me, they have developed a stock-standard answer: "If I knew where the gold was, do you think that I would be %^&*() well working here? And if I knew where it was, do you think that I would $%^&*() tell you about it? I must get asked it at least six times a day during the season."

Migum on Marble Bar Road. I first saw this tree about 18 months earlier and returned on two occasions to try and capture what was a beautiful scene. Each time, the scene looked different. This time, I was fortunate that the spinifex was in flower.

Quartz Circle

A geological phenomenon located about 40 or so kilometres outside of Nullagine. I found it amazing that few people know of its existence. It is every bit as unusual as its "China Wall" counterpart in the Kimberley. Like much of the Pilbara though I suppose, the area around Nullagine has not had the marketing dollars directed toward its promotion: something that will no doubt change in the years to come.

On the Edge of Auriferous Country

The red basalt seen in this photograph represents a country demarcation from the lower-lying schist country. The friend that showed me the location noted that: "On first examination, the rock looks like granite. But when you look at it closely and look to the source rock, it becomes apparent that what you are looking at is very ancient basalt. It is red, rather than the black or grey that you are used to seeing in basalt, because, like much of the Pilbara, it contains traces of iron. This, over time, has oxidised; in other words, the country is rusting."

Donald "Wacka" Wright

Born in Kalgoorlie in 1926, "Wacka" Wright would have to be one of the most interesting and astute people for his age that I have ever met. His nickname "Wacka" is an abbreviated version of "Little Wacka", which was his original nickname: "Me and me mate used to like fight'n' a bit when we were younger. He was older than I was, so he was called "Big Wacka" and me, "Little Wacka". One of his more interesting insights related to detecting the quality of a mine in times past: "You could always tell the quality of a mine by the size of its bottle heap". I then asked him whether he had had any decent sized bottle heaps over the years. He responded: "I always had a bloody big bottle heap, whether there was gold there or not!"

In 1959, Wacka served 12 months at Her Majesty's pleasure when "I got caught up in a bit of a gold racket" treating tellurite recovered from Kalgoorlie's Golden Mile. As tellurite was found only on the Golden Mile, it was illegal for outsiders to be in either possession of the ore (which assayed at around 40 percent gold) or cyanide treating plant. Wacka and his mates were being fed the tellurite by a worker on the Golden Mile and then purifying it before selling it to buyers on boats destined for Singapore and China. He got six months for being in possession of the tellurite and six months for being in possession of the treating plant. Nevertheless, "I must have made about 2,000 quid all up. We didn't have to pay any of it back, and you could buy a new car in those days for 500 quid."

With his late mate Jim Purcell, Wacka took on ownership of the True Blue Mine (near Marble Bar) in September, 1961 for a cost of £5,000 and a deposit of £1! Purcell did not himself have the cash but he had earlier gained a backer through the placement of an advertisement in the paper in his hometown of Kalgoorlie. In 1963, and again with his mate Purcell, Wacka purchased the Kitchener Mine (also near Marble Bar) for £500 cash. This was to prove the richest of the mines with which he was involved. Over the course of two to three years he and Purcell recovered around 1,000 ounces ("which was worth a lot of money in those days") assaying at an average of 10 ounces or more to the ton.

"Wacka" at his old digging, named "Alice", out at the Five Mile outside of Nullagine. Wacka built this camp sometime in the late 1980s to take advantage of a six-acre plot of ground that he had recently acquired. He lived there for at least four years. "I liked the ground. I had a theory that I would hit the jasper bar and make a big splash. Bill Hunter had sunk a shaft right on top of the jasper bar and pulled out 380 ounces".

"Alice" was the wife of "Chum" Alsop who used to have the butcher shop in Nullagine. In building his camp, Wacka got the corrugated iron "wherever I could find it", the black heart timber for the frame "off the black fellas: it took 'em six months to get it to me" and the door off Albert Hanson when he pulled down his shop in Marble Bar ("it must be a hundred years old that door").

Newman

Now a town of some 5,000 people, Newman takes its name from nearby Mt Newman and owes its foundation to the discovery of iron ore by Stan Hilditch on Mt Whaleback in 1957. It was gazetted as a town on 30 June, 1972. Hilditch had been in the area searching for manganese and was later to note:

"When you were in an area you had never been in before, my idea was to get up on the highest hill that I could find, have a good look at the country, see where the water courses were...So I got on top of Whaleback and there it was. I had a look at the structure, and it was obvious from the cut-outs on the south side of Whaleback that it was going to be deep-seated and of high grade. That night I said to Ella: 'This deposit is going to be enormous'".[47]

The Whaleback deposit was to prove to be one of the world's richest and largest single deposits of haematite ore. It assayed at 64% iron content and extended from 240 metres above the surrounding plain, to more than 300 metres below plain level; and this, over a distance of 5.5 kilometres and width of more than 1.5 kilometres.[48] The mine, with its satellite ore-bodies (Ore-bodies 23, 25, 29 and 30, Jimblebar, Yandi, Area C and Yarrie) in 2005 has a productive capacity of around 105 million tonnes per annum[49] and there are still reserves of more than 1.4 billion tonnes of high grade iron: even after more than 25 years of mining.

The Mt Whaleback project was the largest - perhaps even the most difficult - of the Pilbara's four iron ore projects to be launched during the 1960s: the others being Goldsworthy, Tom Price and Cliffs Robe River. This stemmed largely from its distance from the coast - a 426 kilometre railroad was required linking Newman with Nelson Point at Port Hedland. By the time that the railroad was laid it was estimated that the track had been laid at the rate of nearly 240 gallons of beer per kilometre! Elaborate preparations were also required for its port. Though it had been proposed that Mt Whaleback ore should be shipped through Dampier or King Bay, it was ultimately determined that a separate port and railway should be constructed for the Mt Whaleback project. This was to counter the threat of cyclones and would allow customers to have a number of alternate ore sources.[50]

The Mt Whaleback project was launched on 26 June, 1969. Notwithstanding its size, Hilditch and Warman were to receive only a fraction of the rewards that the Hancock and Wright families ultimately received for other similar developments in the Pilbara. A royalty agreement consummated in the late 1970s delivered a total of around A$10M in royalties over the presumed life of the project: 5.42 cents per ton for the first 30 million tons of ore sold, 6.6 cents for the next 70 million tons and 3.3 cents for the following 110 million tons. From there, the rate fell to 0.21 cents for the life of the project.[51]

Mt Whaleback lies in the Ophthalmia Range. The name Mt Whaleback was accorded by Tony Tomich during a drive from the mine site with Stan Hilditch. About 50 kilometres from the site, he turned to Hilditch and asked "Do you mind if I give it a name?" Hilditch responded, "Look, Tony, I don't give a bugger what you call it as long as you give me a good report." "OK, I would like to call it Mt Whaleback", Tomich said. The name, while appropriate, was in fact descriptive of Mt Newman: the hill to which he was erroneously looking and which already had a name.[52]

Sunrise on the Slopes of Mt Newman - Ophthalmia Range

Mt Newman was discovered on 21 August, 1896 by William F. Rudall.[54] It was named by Rudall after Aubrey Newman, the original leader of Rudall's survey party, which was carrying out trigonometrical surveys in the neighbourhood of the Ophthalmia Range in 1896. Newman contracted typhoid fever at Peak Hill and, too ill to continue, was later returned to Cue where he died on May 24th, 1896. I spent four nights on the side of Mt Newman chasing a suitable photograph for this book. On my first day exploring the area, I climbed Mt Newman with 15 kilograms of camera gear in 46^{0}C heat, only to return without making a single photograph.

Evening Storm over the Migums - Ophthalmia Range

One of the more revealing things for my having spent a
full summer down in the Pilbara was the noticeable
change in colour of the bark of the migums. Though
migums are commonly referred to as "snappy gums" in
the Pilbara, migum is their correct name. Snappy gums
are generally only found further north in the Kimberley.
Typically, and like the snappy gum, the migum is found in
range country and along rocky ridges.[55]

Iron Country - Kalgan Pool - Kalgan Creek - Ophthalmia Range

Kalgan Creek was first traversed by William Rudall in September, 1896 but not named until much later. Surveyor, Bocksette in 1960, confirmed that it was locally known as "Kulga Creek" and not "Kalgan Creek".[56]

Located in the Ophthalmia Range, Three Pools is a
beautiful, but difficult, place at which to compose a
photograph. I was unable to identify when it was
discovered, though it obviously takes its name from the
existence of three cascading pools.

Depending upon who one talks to, Wanna Munna has one of three meanings. The first is that Wunna Munna means "picking up stick". The Nyiyaparli people of the Ophthalmia Range area use the word "munna" when referring to one's backside! Finally, the Martu people don't use the word "munna" in their everyday language. The word "wunna" though is used in their language to denote "digging stick". [57] Newman local, John Flint, once held an active mining lease at Wanna Munna, not far from the petroglyth site, and was mining copper and other related minerals. The mine shafts are still there and care should be taken when walking in the area.

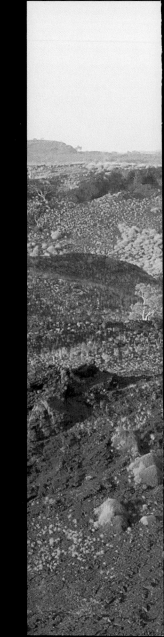

I was shown this spot by Joe Farulyas of <u>Pilbara Iron Country Tours (0419 967 568)</u>. Joe runs a 4WD tag-a-long tour service around Newman and his knowledge of the country, gained over 20 or more years in the area, is first-rate. It would be hard to meet more genuine people than he and his wife, Maria.

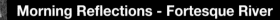

Morning Reflections - Fortesque River

I nearly didn't see the opportunity for this photograph. On rising from my sleep, and unable to see a shot worth taking, I decided to go for a swim and early morning wash in the river nearby. This was my reward. The Fortesque River was discovered by Francis Gregory on 29 May, 1861. It was named after "the Under Secretary of State for the

Electrical Storm over Mt Whaleback[59]

The exact processes that give rise to lightning are still the subject of much heated (pardon the pun) debate. It is thought that negative ions accumulate near the base of the thundercloud making that area of the cloud negatively charged. As the cloud moves above the surface of the earth, the ground immediately below the cloud becomes positively charged (opposite charges are drawn to one another). As air is an excellent insulator, the two opposites at first cannot meet. The result is that a huge electric potential is created until such time that the air cannot hold back the negative electrons any longer. A surge of electrons rushes down to the cloud base and then on toward the ground.

The surge of electrons does not flow continuously. Rather the process occurs in a series of steps, racing down at a speed of about 220,000 kilometres per hour for 50 - 100 metres before stopping for something like one fifty millionth of a second and continuing on for another 50 - 100 metres, etc. As the electrons approach the ground, positive ions move up from the ground through protruding objects such as trees, antennas, even human beings. When they meet, a strong electric current moves up into the cloud along a channel a few centimetres wide. It is this return stroke that is visible to the human eye, though, its direction, due to the speed of movement, is not discernable.

Because lightning is so incredibly hot - at 30,000°C it is some five times hotter than the surface of the sun - the surrounding air expands explosively. It is these shockwaves that we hear as thunder. As a general rule, for every three seconds that elapse between a lightning strike and its associated thunder, the strike is one kilometre away. However, one can still be at risk of a strike even if the storm is 10 kilometres away.

This photograph was taken during one of the Pilbara's driest summers in many years. I had initially driven to the top of Radio Hill to photograph an earlier electrical storm but left to get some dinner when I "decided" that the bolts were not overly spectacular. About an hour later, and as I left the restaurant, lightning bolts electrified the sky at a rate that I had not often seen. I raced to the top of Radio Hill and shot the storm before torrential rain necessitated a dash for my vehicle.

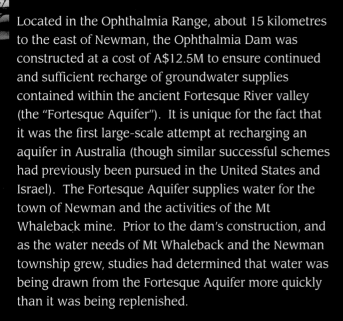

Ophthalmia Dam - Fortesque River

Located in the Ophthalmia Range, about 15 kilometres to the east of Newman, the Ophthalmia Dam was constructed at a cost of A$12.5M to ensure continued and sufficient recharge of groundwater supplies contained within the ancient Fortesque River valley (the "Fortesque Aquifer"). It is unique for the fact that it was the first large-scale attempt at recharging an aquifer in Australia (though similar successful schemes had previously been pursued in the United States and Israel). The Fortesque Aquifer supplies water for the town of Newman and the activities of the Mt Whaleback mine. Prior to the dam's construction, and as the water needs of Mt Whaleback and the Newman township grew, studies had determined that water was being drawn from the Fortesque Aquifer more quickly than it was being replenished.

At flood storage capacity, Ophthalmia Dam holds approximately 26 million cubic metres of water (about $\frac{1}{19}$th the size of Sydney Harbour). However, only three million cubic metres of this is permanent due to the area's average annual evaporation of around three metres. The Dam incorporates three separate earth walls that have a combined length of nearly four kilometres and a maximum height of 12 metres. The main spillway is 580 metres long. How much area the water covers - the Dam's average depth is three metres - depends upon the bounty of the annual Wet season and the levels of the aquifers.

From Ophthalmia Dam, water is fed to natural or artificial recharge areas where the soils allow it to reach the aquifers quickly: thus overcoming the previous problems of water loss through Wet season run-off and evaporation. Another purpose of the Dam is to allow silt to settle so that clean water can be drawn off. For this reason, recreational activity is limited to sailing and canoeing and no activities that could create muddy conditions are permitted (for example, the use of outboard motors).

Ophthalmia Dam takes its name from the nearby Ophthalmia Range, which was discovered and named by Ernest Giles on 18 May, 1876. His diary notes:

"At night my eyes were so much inflamed and so painful with ophthalmia, that I could scarcely see... From what Alec saw and described to me, it was evident that we were upon the edge of the desert, as if the ranges ceased to the east, it was not likely that any watercourses could exist without them. No watercourses could be seen in any direction, except that from which we had come. It was a great disappointment to me to get such information, as I had hoped to discover some creeks or rivers that might carry me some distance farther eastward; but now it was evident they did not exist. I called this range, whose almost western end Alec ascended, Ophthalmia Range, in consequence of my suffering so much from that frightful malady."[60]

Murray and Ray Kennedy - Roy Hill Station

Murray and Ray Kennedy moved to the Pilbara from Kalgoorlie to take up the Millstream Station lease with their father in 1964. In 1972 they purchased Roy Hill Station - "we got wind that trouble was brewing" - in anticipation of the possible resumption of Millstream by the State. Both stations at the time of their acquisition were stocked with sheep; primarily because of labour problems to do with drunks and staff "finding excuses not to work". Their father worked Roy Hill and Murray and Ray, Millstream, though they did assist their father at mustering time. In 1982, and "after a 14 year fight", the government "got nasty" and put out a resumption order on Millstream. "They tried every dirty bloody thing in the book to get rid of us" - [including the running of nearby V8 heavy engines during the night to keep them awake] - but still managed to ride the turmoil and negotiate double the resumption price that had originally been offered. Their father died in 1985 and is now buried on the side of the hill from which the station takes its name. Murray noted: "He didn't like the city. He reckoned they [the people there] smelt; stunk. They do too!"

Today, in the latter part of their lives, and unable to withstand the physical rigours demanded by the annual muster, the bulk of Murray and Ray's time is taken up by another challenge: identifying the reasons behind the mysterious, but widespread, deaths of significant stands of coolabah and mulga; both on their property and in other parts of the east Pilbara. Though the cause of this vegetation loss has not yet been scientifically established, Murray and Ray believe these deaths to be the result of a combination of water and air-borne pollutants; possibly attributable to upstream mining activities. They theorise that vegetation deaths outside the Fortesque catchment area, most notably to the south and south-east of Newman, are attributable to air-borne pollutants. Opponents to this position, of which there are many, attribute these deaths to overgrazing. Whichever view is the correct one, a sighting of this vegetation loss reveals it to be more than just an isolated occurrence. It is hoped that an independent study, which is due to be released shortly after the publication of this book, will shed further light on what is a concerning issue. If the problem is not attributable to natural causes, one would hope that steps could be taken to provide redress.

I rolled into Roy Hill Station in February, 2005 not quite knowing what to expect. I had been warned by one individual to ring before going there, "as they wear guns and they will use them!". As I was to learn, this was a significant exaggeration and, according to Murray, "a character assassination by the mining industry". It would be hard to find more genuine people. Jayne, Murray's partner, did note however (and quite seriously) that "I had to bite the bullet one day and told them that all guns and hats were to be put on the fridge before they sit down to eat at the table".

My time spent at Roy Hill was an enjoyable one. Though I had intended to stay, at most a night, I ended up staying a couple of days and was fascinated by the eccentricities of Murray and Ray and by the authenticity and antiquity of the station buildings. A key thing that I was to learn related to an unusual interpretation of what appeared to be a straight-forward enough comment. Ray noted, during one conversation, that: "Excuse me for a minute. I have to go and see someone about a dog." Translated by Murray's partner, Jayne, I later learnt that this in fact meant "I have to go to the toilet!" I also learned that their basis for not living in the main homestead related to their concern for the fact that it got flooded with 18 inches of water back in 1946. This has lead to the installation of a series of dongas mounted on stilts at the homestead's rear. These are linked by narrow universal steel beams (you feel like you are walking the plank) which act as walkways and which are named after people that have fallen off them. "Bill's Leap" was named when "Bill went out in the dark and fell over the edge". "Michael's Drop" was named when Michael was carrying an air-conditioner, failed to look where he was going, and ended up flat on his back, four foot below, wearing an air-conditioner on his chest!"

Coolabah Reflections - Fortesque River

The white-barked coolabah *(Eucalyptus victrix)* seen here is one of three main species found along most Pilbara watercourses. Typically, coolabahs are located back from the river-red-gums *(Eucalyptus camaldulensis)* and melaleucas *(Melaleuca leucodendron)* that line the banks of major watercourses. White-barked eucalypts found in smaller watercourses are nearly always coolabahs. This is the dominant coolabah, though a grey-barked relation is found in the Kimberley region.

Karijini National Park

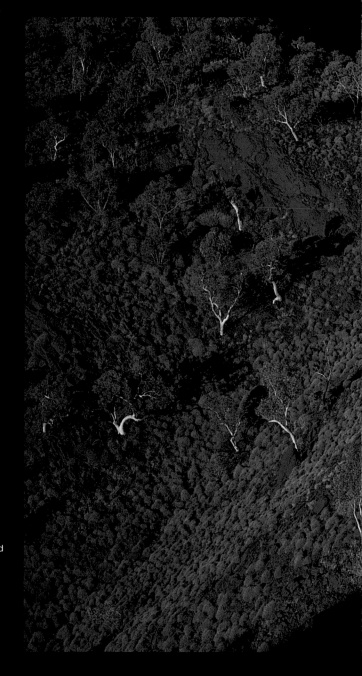

Karijini National Park falls within the Hamersley Range and, at 627,444 hectares, is Western Australia's second largest National Park. It was gazetted in 1969. The Hamersley Range was discovered by Francis Gregory on 6th June, 1861 during his expedition to explore the North-West "as a preliminary to actual settlement".[61] It was named after Edward Hamersley "one of the most liberal promoters of the expedition"[62] and incorporates Western Australia's two highest peaks, Mt Meharry (1,245m) and Mt Bruce (1,235m). Mt Bruce was discovered also by Gregory on 3 July, 1861 and accorded its name "after the gallant commander of the troops, who has always warmly supported me in carrying out explorations".[63]

It is thought that the formation of the Hamersley commenced around 2.77 billion years ago. Then, the Pilbara was part of a single continent, the "Pilbara Continent". Over a period of 80 million years, the Pilbara Continent stretched and two continents (the Pilbara and Yilgarn) were created. These were separated by a small ocean, the floor of which was created by basaltic lava flows that had erupted to the surface during the separation.[64]

Despite it being chemically identical to sandstone, chert, one of the layers in the banded iron formation, is almost completely insoluble in its purest form and is completely stable under atmospheric conditions: in other words, it is very hard. It is this resistance to erosion that causes the banded iron formation to break off in large chunks - usually where water has eroded along fractures or joints - and creates the distinctive scarp country that is so evident in the Hamersley Range.

Chert, in its pure state, is constituted by a perfectly interlocking, and reinforcing, matrix. It is formed at the bottom of deep seas as a chemical sediment in places where there is virtually no water movement and where there is volcanic activity. Sandstone, on the other hand, is created by the weathering and erosion of surface rocks that contain quartz. [67]

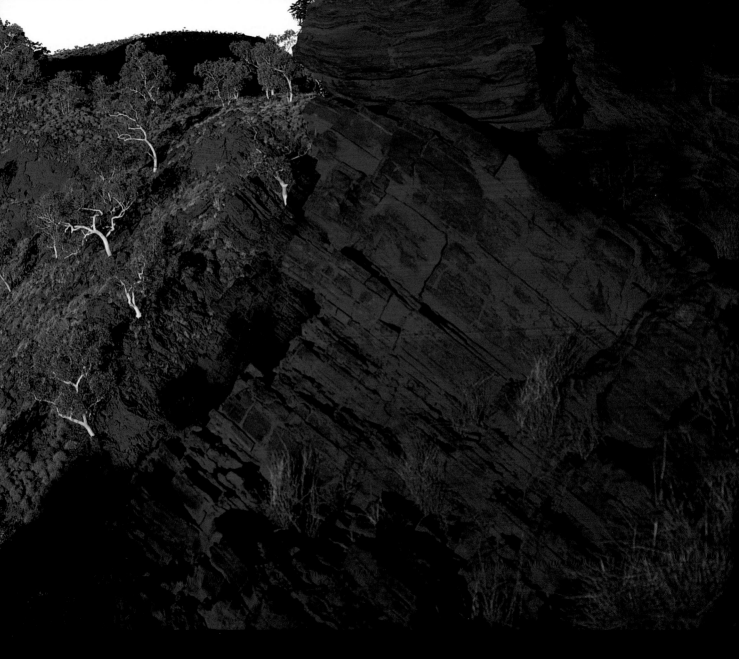

2.47 to 2.69 billion years ago, the ocean separating the Pilbara and Yilgarn continents was characterised by high levels of silica (SiO2) and, at periods, pulses of iron (Fe2+). These were produced by volcanic activity and weathering. At this time, the atmosphere had little or no oxygen. Gradually, it is thought, cyanobacteria, the earth's first living organisms, perfected photosynthesis. Oxygen was released as a by-product to in turn react with the iron salts in the water. These produced insoluble ferric oxides that crystallised and sank to the seabed to create the banded iron layers (part of the banded iron formation) that predominate throughout the Hamersley Range.[65]

Seen from a distance, the colour of the bands within the banded iron formation are not a reliable guide as to their mineralisation: small amounts of impurities can create disproportionate discolouration. Chert (silica), for example, in its purest form is naturally clear. However, chert layers, when incorporating other minerals, can take any one of a number of colours (black, red, yellow, brown, etc.) depending upon the nature of the impurity. The same can be said for banded iron layers; the colour of which will also be determined by the type of any impurities. The "scratch" test is therefore one of the more reliable indicators for determining whether a layer is haematitic (ie, iron ore). If a scratching of the rock reveals it to be cherry-red underneath, then the rock is almost certainly iron ore (even if it does have an alternate surface colouration).

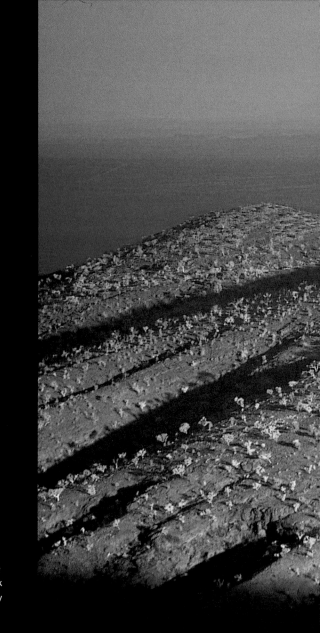

Sunset from Mt Meharry - Hamersley Range

Mt Meharry was discovered by Surveyor Trevor Markey and his party in 1967. It was named after the late Mr W.T. Meharry, Chief Geodetic Surveyor who died on 16 May, 1967 at the age of 54.[68] The access track is extremely steep and rough and has the potential to be dangerous for inexperienced "off-roaders". I say this as I sit atop the mountain itself, having watched a Landcruiser ute, from a nearby mining company, fail to negotiate its sheet rock and steep gradient earlier this afternoon.

1.6 - 2.2 billion years ago, the Pilbara and Yilgarn continents collided. The resultant buckling and folding led to the creation of a major mountain range; perhaps 10,000 metres in height. It is the eroded remnants that are today evident as the Hamersley Range.[66] Today, the Pilbara Craton and Yilgarn are sutured together as a single unit and form part of the geologically stable Australia-India Plate.

The Hamersley Range is characterised by high red ridges and escarpments and can be distinguished from the more rounded ranges of the Ashburton Basin which lie to its south. This stems from a number of factors. First, and most significantly, the core of the Pilbara Craton is buoyant: held up by a thick lithospheric keel. This is a deep, cold, part of the mantle directly underlying the earth's crust (or surface), which is depleted of heat producing elements and is relatively light and buoyant. It is this process that has kept the Pilbara Craton at about the level of the present day through almost the entirety of its 3.5 billion year history. Second, the banded iron formation is far more resistant to erosion than the clays, siltstones and dolomites that are more dominant in the Ashburton Basin.

Reflections from Down Below - Joffre Gorge

Joffre Gorge is Karijini's longest, deepest, and one of its wettest, gorge systems. It was originally named Bismarck Creek by surveyor T. Beasley but altered to its current name (after General Joffre) in 1914 due to the war with Germany. [73]

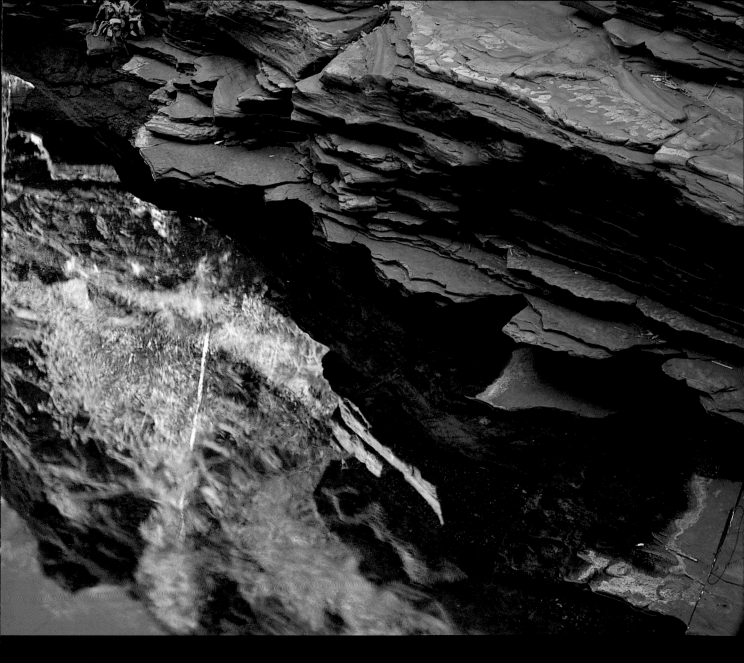

Junction Pool viewed from Oxer's Lookout

At Junction Pool, Hancock, Joffre, Red and Weano Gorges intersect to afford one of Australia's most spectacular gorge vistas. Oxer's Lookout takes its name from Dr Gordon Oxer of Wittenoom who, during the 1960s was the town doctor, operator of the Wittenoom Chalet and the Chairman of the Wittenoom Tourist and Progress Association.[69] Angular gorge junctions, such as that at Junction Pool, occur where two or more directions of jointing are present.

Reflected Light - Weano Gorge

Weano Gorge was named by Dr Gordon Oxer in 1962 after an Aboriginal man named Weano, who, around 1936, had shown Leo Snell the way into Yampire Gorge. Snell discovered asbestos in Yampire Gorge and Weano is credited as having therefore given rise to the asbestos industry in the Hamersley Range.[70] Like nearby Hancock Gorge, the many undercut areas of this gorge have been created by the abrasive action of water and debris eroding softer rock layers (for example, tuffs, shales and carbonates) at a faster rate than the more resistant banded iron formation.[71]

The Beauty of Mother Nature - Hancock Gorge

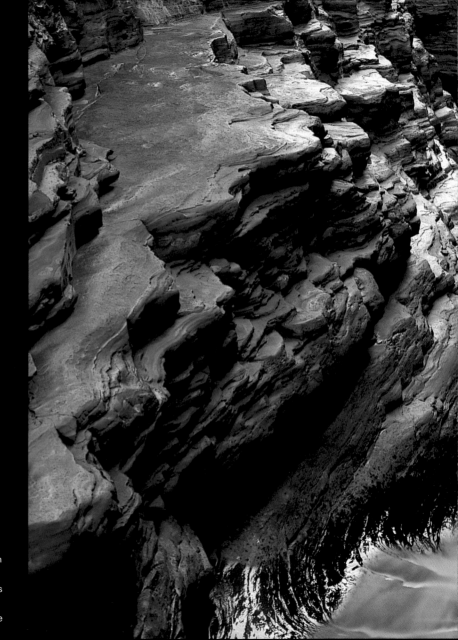

Hancock Gorge, like each of the major gorges in Karijini, has been formed where turbulent fast-flowing water, often associated with cyclones and tropical depressions, has combined with rock debris to erode the banded iron formation and cap-rock along vertical and horizontal joints. It takes its name from George Hancock, one of the late partners in Mulga Downs Station.[72]

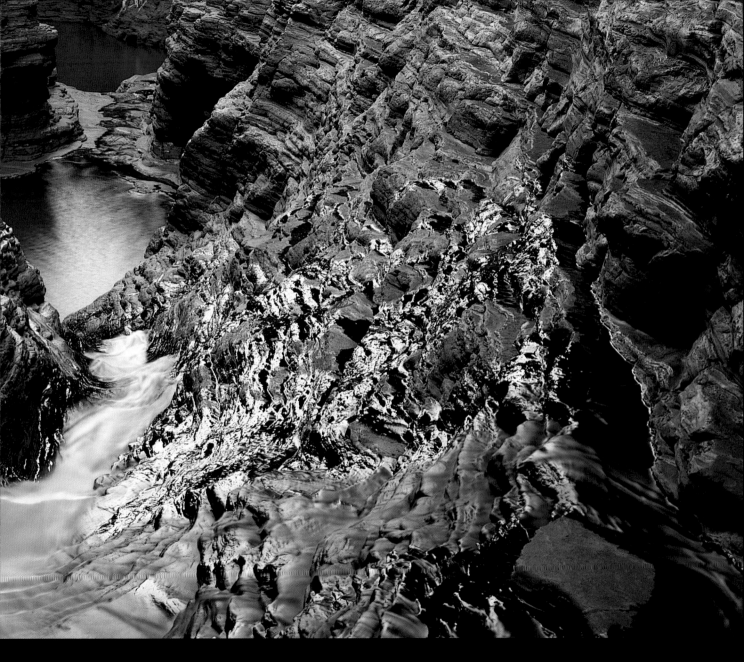

A Hidden Oasis - Fern Pool - Dale's Gorge

The waterfall at Fern Pool is one of the more beautiful that I have seen in Australia. A delicate maiden-hair fern habitat lies near its base and care should be taken to avoid its disturbance.

Fortesque Falls - Dale's Gorge

Access to the Karijini gorges was provided initially via the construction of a track from Wittenoom through Yampire Gorge. The track was pioneered by Dr Gorden Oxer of Wittenoom. This track has since been closed on the back of concerns that the existence of blue asbestos within the gorge affords a health risk.

Pushing the Limits - The Gauntlet - Knox Gorge

This photograph involved considerable danger to life, but I wanted something that was different to other photos taken at this same place. Fortunate to be in the park as rain teamed down, I shot down Knox Gorge at 0700 in case the Park was closed. Karijini gorges are particularly susceptible to flash-flooding due to their narrow width, non-porous catchment areas and the fact that rain typically falls heavily in concentrated periods. One local I was later to talk with indicated that he had seen water levels in this gorge rise by 10 metres in a matter of three minutes.

The above, combined with the very real risk of falling, were right at the forefront of my mind as I pushed down toward the location of this photograph. Basically, I was as nervous as hell. In dry weather, one is always nervous down here, let alone during a heavy rain-bearing depression (the walls of the Karijini gorges are slippery even in dry weather)! Suspended above a sharply dropping waterfall (legs pushing against one wet gorge wall and my back against the other wet gorge wall to keep me from falling) with camera, tripod and light-metre around my neck, my body tremoured as I manually counted out what was a seven minute exposure. My Akubra acted as my umbrella and I guessed the exposure: the light was simply too dark for my light metre to register.

Knox Gorge was named by Dr Gordon Oxer after Sir Edward Knox, one of the early chiefs of the Colonial Sugar Refining Company. The Colonial Sugar Refining Company, through its subsidiary, Australian Blue Asbestos Ltd, held the asbestos leases in Wittenoom and Yampire Gorges during the 1960s.[74]

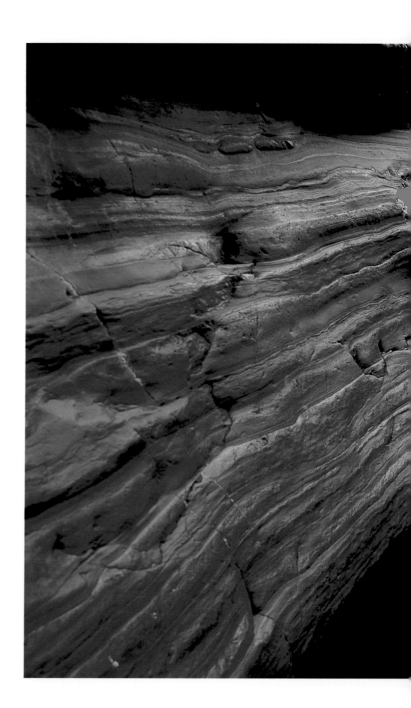

The Power of Mother Nature - Hamersley Gorge

Hamersley Gorge is perhaps my favourite gorge within Karijini; purely because it is so different to any other gorge that I have seen. The bottom of the gorge is comprised of banded iron formation and slate with some minor sandstone beds and dolerite; the slate being particularly obvious on the eastern side of the river and on the western side near Spa Pool. Slate is a weakly metamorphosed mudstone. The massive grey layer of rock that underlies the banded iron formation, and that is at its most spectacular on the eastern side, is dolerite.

The eastern wall shows the banded iron formation give way to a combination of layered and softer, white, yellow, orange, even purple-coloured rock. This runs parallel to, and is layered the same as, the underlying banded iron formation. It was originally a banded iron formation also, but has been affected by intense surface weathering that is a feature over much of the Pilbara region. This surface weathering has effectively reduced, and removed, much of the iron from the rocks and weathered the remainder to clays.[75]

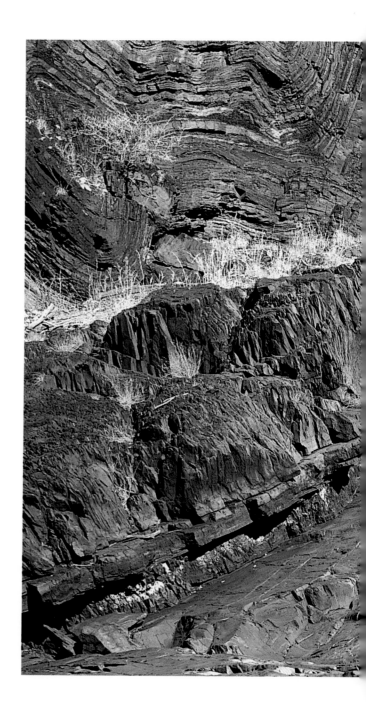

Intense surface weathering is slowly dissolving the banded iron formation of the western wall near the base of the access steps.[76] On my last visit there, I was disappointed to see the work of one "peanut" who had etched his name into the rock.

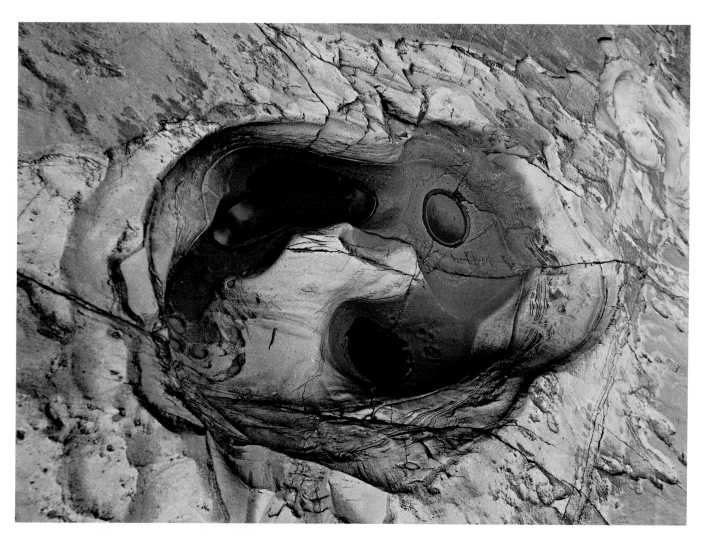

Rock Patterns - Hamersley Gorge

Every visit to Hamersley Gorge yields new angles and photographic
opportunities, as seen in this photograph of an evaporating rock-pool.

Spa Pool - Hamersley Gorge

Two fern species survive on the walls of Spa Pool. These species are also present in greater abundance at Dales Gorge where the gorge sides provide a suitable habitat, in addition, for a trailing trigger plant not seen in the other gorges.

Karijini Wildlife

Karijini is home to a diverse range of flora and fauna, though species diversity tends to be higher in the Park's gorges and low-lying areas due to the greater habitat diversity. It is estimated that the Park is home to some 750 - 800 flowering plant species. To date, at least 30 mammal species, 133 bird species, 90 reptile and amphibian species and 8 fish species have been found within the Park. Between the months of March and August, the rare Peregrine Falcon has also been sighted in the Park's gorge cliff faces. It is further thought that, with intensive searching, bilby populations might be found (though at present, they are thought to be extinct within the Park).[77]

Karijini National Park also has a healthy dingo population. It is one of the few areas within Western Australia where it is feasible to protect dingoes which, and while a pest under the Agriculture and Related Resources Protection Act 1976, are protected on CALM managed estate. Thought to have been introduced 4,000 - 5,000 years ago, there is evidence that the presence of dingoes helps to minimise fox and cat populations. This in turn has a beneficial impact on native fauna populations.[78]

I was greeted with this rarely witnessed sight in February, 2004 while exiting Hancock Gorge. A Pilbara Olive Python had only recently swallowed a large marsupial (possibly a wallaby) and was going to be restricted from movement for up to two weeks while its digestive processes went about their work.

Tom Price and Surrounds

Located in the western part of the Hamersley Range, the town of Tom Price takes its name from nearby Mt Tom Price, the site of one of Hamersley Iron's largest iron ore mines. Mt Tom Price was named after the Vice President of Kaiser Steel, one of two joint venture companies that mining giant Rio Tinto combined with to form Hamersley Holdings. Hamersley Holdings was the operating company established to develop the massive iron ore deposits that had been located and pegged by station-owner, and part-time prospector, Lang Hancock in the 1950s and early 1960s. Mining operations commenced at Tom Price in 1966.

Up on the "Hill" – Mt Tom Price

Though Lang Hancock was responsible for the identification of many of the Hamersley Range's major iron ore deposits, discovery of the massive Tom Price deposit was made by Zinc Corporation geologists, Bill Burns and Ian Whitchers. Hancock and Rio Tinto Senior Geologist, Bruno Campana, had identified it as a good prospect but had been unable to land due to the nature of the terrain.

Hancock's discoveries saw him become one of Australia's richest men. With his business partner, E.A. Wright, he negotiated a 2.5% royalty on the value of each ton of ore exported. This applied not only to discoveries that he and McCamey had made, but also on any additional deposits that Hamersley might later mine. The rationale was that Rio had taken up reserves on only a fraction of the deposits they had been introduced to by Hancock and the remainder might be developed later. By 1979, Hancock and Wright were receiving A$50,000 per day in royalties.[84]

Though it had been recognised that the Pilbara was home to vast reserves of iron ore much earlier than the 1950s, the significance of their discovery at the time was limited. In 1898, government geologist Harvey Woodward had noted that: "There is enough [iron ore] to supply the whole world should present supplies run out...but as iron ores are of no value it is useless to trouble about them."[79] Hancock's "arrival" was significant in two respects. First, he was to locate world-class ore deposits where magnetometer surveys, previously undertaken by BHP and the West Australian Department of Mines, had failed.[80] Magnetometer surveys were dependent, for their efficacy, on the detection of magnetic field *anomalies*. These were not present on the basis that high-grade haematite existed throughout the entire range. Steady overall graphs produced by the surveys were wrongly interpreted to mean that there was no iron: instead, the converse was true.

Country "Alive" – Hamersley Range – near Tom Price

It took me three visits to this, one of my favourite Hamersley Range locations, before I captured some photographs with which I was satisfied. Technical difficulties with a new piece of camera equipment rendered my early efforts unsatisfactory (I'm opposed to the ever-increasing tendency toward artificial manipulation of images and would rather get the original transparency right). The Hamersley's prevalent banded iron formation is clearly evident in the exposed foreground rock.

Hancock's identification of these rich iron ore deposits coincided with growing global steel-mill demand for high-grade iron ore. Questioned about their discovery, he was later to note:

"I was flying down south with my wife Hope [from their station in the Chichester Ranges to Perth in November, 1952], and we left a bit later than usual and by the time we got over the Hamersley Ranges, the clouds had formed and the ceiling got lower and lower. I got into the Turner River, knowing full well if I followed it through, I would come out into the Ashburton. On going through the gorge in the Turner River, I noticed that the walls looked to me to be solid iron and was particularly alerted by the rusty looking colour of it, it showed to me to be oxidised iron".[81]

Hancock returned after his trip to Perth and flew back to the gorges that had afforded him "protection" from the November storms. He landed on unprepared ground, in spinifex country, on mesas, in gorges and in places to which no other vehicle had been. He gathered ore samples over a stretch of 50 miles or more and sent them to Perth to be assayed. "[T]o my surprise they were 2% higher than the standard blast furnace feed in the mightiest nation on earth, the United States, so I knew that it was not only large, but it was high grade."[82] When the Commonwealth lifted its embargo on the exportation of iron ore (refer Port Hedland text) on 29 March, 1961, Hancock had men waiting undercover in gorges across the breath of the Hamersley. They pegged his claims in dramatic fashion, using fire to ignite the spinifex.[83]

During the early days in Tom Price, all sorts of games were played. A former local – who asked not to be named!!! - noted: "We used to get up to all sorts of tricks with Hamersley Iron. I was a loader driver and each evening all the drivers would meet to synchronise their watches. Then, when we were due to start our shift the next day, we would all start up at the same time. With all the sudden drain on power, the power plant could not handle it and so the power plant would be knocked out for about four hours. Because we were all members of the Federated Engine Drivers' Union, we were not allowed to be deployed to other tasks and we effectively got four hours off. Eventually, Hamersley wised up and we were not allowed to start up our machines until authorised in sequence by the company."

McCamey's Iron Tree – Hamersley Range – near Tom Price

McCamey's Iron Tree was another of the indicators that Lang Hancock used to locate the Pilbara's high-grade iron deposits. The iron tree lives in rock crevices created by millennia of leaching. The existence of leaching points to the possible existence of iron and, in Hancock's case, suggested ground that was worthy of further investigation.[85]

Sunrise Glow – Migum – Hamersley Range – near Tom Price

One of the challenges with photographing alone is that one needs always to be conscious of safety. This necessitates that one take precautions for what are ordinarily the simplest of tasks. Nowadays I carry my survival kit, space blanket, satellite phone and crepe bandages for even the shortest of walks. In places, such as the location in which this photograph was taken, snake-bite, or the rolling of an ankle, can easily prove fatal.

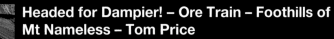

Headed for Dampier! – Ore Train – Foothills of Mt Nameless – Tom Price

Ore trains throughout the Pilbara are typically about two kilometres long and incorporate at least 200 carriages and at least two locomotives. It is not uncommon to be stuck at a level crossing for five to ten minutes waiting for a train to pass; especially if you arrive just as the locomotives at the train's front go past. On 21 June, 2001, BHP Iron Ore set world records for the longest and heaviest train. The train measured 7.353 kilometres in length, carried 82,262.5 tonnes of ore, involved 682 ore cars and 8 locomotives, and travelled 275 kilometres from BHP Iron Ore's Newman and Yandi mines to Port Hedland.[86]

Mt Nameless was originally named Mt No Name by a Hamersley Iron survey team, before common usage saw its name changed to Mt Nameless.[87] I spent in excess of nine hours, over a period of two days, waiting for this photograph.

Paraburdoo and Surrounds

Paraburdoo is very much a mining town and is not geared for tourists. There is no caravan park or visitor centre and some of the better spots are inaccessible due to them being located on mining leases. Notwithstanding, the Paraburdoo landscape is interesting and, in places, stunning. The town itself sits near the intersection of the Hamersley Range and Ashburton Basin amidst what is a very clear country change.

Construction of the Paraburdoo township and mine commenced in 1970, though production at the wholly-owned Paraburdoo Mine was delayed until the first quarter of 1973 due to a slowdown in the Japanese economy. The nearby Channar Mine commenced production in January, 1990 and represents a 60:40 joint venture with the Chinese-owned Sino-Steel. The Eastern Range project, a 54:46 joint venture with Shanghai-based Baosteel Group, commenced production in April, 2004.[88]

Paraburdoo Mine - Paraburdoo

The name Paraburdoo was accorded to prevent confusion with a nearby creek and station property that was called Piraburdoo. It is widely thought that the name Piraburdoo was derived by the early settlers from the Aboriginal term "piru-pardu" (meaning feathered meat) after flocks of galahs that frequented the trees of a nearby creek on that station.

However, research by former Westrac employee, Noel Austin, suggests that there is an alternate meaning. He notes, from the archives of the Western Australian State Library, that "[O]riginally, the post office, following a ruling by the Nomenclature Committee, adopted the spelling of Pirraburdu. [This is similar to the name of] the nearby station, which has existed since 1916 and means Place of Ochre. As from 1970 the official name was adopted as Paraburdoo".[90]

Together, the three mines, operated by Pilbara Iron as the Greater Paraburdoo operation, produced around 18 million tonnes of iron ore in the year ended 30 June, 2004. However, production numbers will continue to rise as Eastern Range provides full-year figures and Chinese demand rises strongly. Ore from the Channar and Eastern Range operations are transported to Paraburdoo by conveyor where they are processed and blended and then loaded onto a waiting train. The iron content of the Paraburdoo/ Eastern Range projects averages 63% iron, and the Channar deposit, around 61.5%.[89]

Eucalypt Burl – Bellary Creek – Tom Price-Paraburdoo Road

This 30 kilometre-long creek caught my eye during a drive from Tom Price to Paraburdoo. I returned over two nights to ensure that I captured the image that I wanted. Bellary Creek appears to have first been traversed by A.J. Bennett in August, 1921.[91]

As is the case with many of the towns in Australia's north, Paraburdoo has its share of humorous tales. A former local, who wished not to be named, relayed his experience while working on the local hospital during the 1960s and 1970s. Temperatures during that project were in the low to mid 40s and refrigeration was not as readily available as it is today. He noted: "I found out that the only fridge there at the hospital was the one they had at the morgue. So I headed down to the morgue, and when I opened up the fridge found that there was a "stiff" inside. I pulled out the body – it hadn't yet been identified – wacked the beer in the fridge and thought nothing more of it. Anyway, a couple of hours later, the Matron bailed me up and grabbed me by the throat. She was ready to kill me, but I got away with it." Another local spoke of an incident involving a contract tradesman: "This guy was working on a project at the school. Anyway, he kept wrecking doors – he didn't mean to – and said that if he wrecked another one, he would head up to the top of Radio Hill [a prominent hill overlooking the town] and chuck it over the side. That's why, if you look closely, you can see a door halfway down the side of Radio Hill."

Reflections – Nanjilgardy Pool – Turee Creek

This waterhole is inaccessible now due to the access road passing through a nearby mining lease. It is a beautiful pool of permanent water in a generally dry region. This pool was surveyed and named by A.J. Bennett in August, 1920.[92]

Geology and Vegetation of the Ashburton Basin

The landscapes and vegetation of the Ashburton Basin form an almost total contrast to those of the Hamersley Range to its immediate, and proximate, north. The very obvious vegetation differences between these regions are thought to be attributable to variances in temperatures, or winter rainfall, rather than geology.[3]

The Ashburton Basin was not part of the Yilgarn Craton but is directly attached to the southern margin of the Pilbara Craton and overlays rocks of the older Hamersley Basin. The younger rocks of the Ashburton Basin are dominated by rocks deposited on top of, and along the margins of, the Pilbara Craton and include sandstone, siltstone and dolomite. Because there was little heat input in this area there are few volcanic rocks (with the exception of the top layers of the Ashburton Basin) and little banded iron formation. The Ashburton Basin is itself overlain by rocks of the Bangemall Basin, so the whole series documents a progressive build-up of sediment on the edge of the Pilbara Craton over a long period of time.[4]

As I indicated earlier, I find that the best time to photograph a place is when the light appears to be at its worst. The key factor I believe is to ensure that you are "in position" in case something does happen. This photograph reflects the advantages of this approach, though I had only a 30 second window to work with. It is these 30 second-type windows that represent my photograph "nirvana".

Another sunrise photograph taken near Paraburdoo in the vicinity of Turee Creek. As may be apparent to some in this photograph, the Ashburton Basin is characterised by a more rounded, and lower lying, topography than that of the Hamersley Range to the north. The more rounded topography is attributable to the existence of softer sandstone, siltstone and dolomite which tends to weather more evenly. Its lower topography stems from the fact that the core of the Pilbara Craton, which is overlain by the Hamersley and Chichester Ranges to the north, is buoyant (see earlier discussion of the geology of the Hamersley Range).

Spines of the Short-Beaked Echidna *(Tachyglossus aculeatus).*

I saw this animal on the Ningaloo coast after finishing a morning shoot in the sand dunes. With the platypus, the echidna is one of two egg-laying mammals. Their spines are made of hair and they are long-lived, reaching up to 49 years in captivity. They are possibly Australia's most widely distributed mammal.

The Black Headed Python *(Aspidites melanocephalus)*.

This animal we found in the Ashburton Basin in the Turee Creek catchment area south-east of Paraburdoo. They are burrowing snakes and can often be found with just their head above-ground. It is thought that the black colour of their head may enable them to absorb heat and increase their body-temperature without exposing their whole body. It may also act as camouflage when hunting for prey.

Like Paraburdoo to its south-east, Pannawonica is a mining town. It is dedicated to the service of the Robe River iron ore operations. One should not visit with the expectation of seeing a visitor centre or finding a wide range of interpretive material, though the locals are helpful. Construction of the Pannawonica township, mine, plant and Wickham port all commenced in 1970, following the 1969 signing of initial sales contracts between the Robe River Joint Venture and the Japanese steel mills. These sales contracts were the largest iron ore sales agreements in the world to that time and amounted to some A$1.37B in 1969 terms.[95] The town itself was gazetted on 30 June, 1972.[96]

Mesa J – Robe River Iron Associates - Pannawonica

Around five trains a day, averaging 196 – 204 carriages in length, depart Mesa J, the site of Pilbara Iron's current Robe operations. Each carriage carts around 100 tonnes of ore and a two kilometre-long train is fully loaded and turned around in about three and a half hours.[100]

Although Robe River iron ore is of a lower grade than that of other Hamersley Range iron operations (averaging 57% compared to 62% for the average haematite ores of the Hamersley Range)[97], its construction was undertaken to fulfil a niche in the range of Japanese steel mills' blast furnace options. It also allowed an ideal opportunity for the more orderly exploitation of Western Australia's iron ore resources, via the supply of both high and low grade ore to world markets. Initial participation in the Robe River Joint Venture involved no less than seven participants, spread in varying proportions of 40%, 30% and 30% Australian, American and Japanese interests. The first shipment of sinter fines from Cape Lambert took place in October, 1972, with the inaugural cargo of pellets following in December of the same year.[98]

Looking down the Robe River Valley - Pannawonica

The Robe mesas stand an average of 50 metres above the surrounding plains. They run in roughly an east-west direction to a distance of some 34 kilometres east of the Pannawonica townsite.[101] This photograph, taken at sunrise, shows the distinctive mesas of the Robe Valley in the background.

A Contrast in Colour – Robe River - Pannawonica

Each of the major Pilbara iron ore mines are different. As noted in the text,
the Robe River mesas incorporate pisolite, rather than haematite, ore. They
are therefore shallower than the ore found at Mt Whaleback or Tom Price and
the mine, at 12 kilometres in length, is much longer than the deeper five
kilometre – long Mt Whaleback hole at Newman. The pool adjacent to this
cliff was first referred to by H.S. Carey in 1878. It is one of many beautiful
pools along the Robe River.[102]

The ore of the Robe River valley is pisolitic, rather than haematitic, iron ore. Pisolitic ore generally consists of a combination of the iron minerals goethite and haematite and a small amount of clay and silica. The Robe River system began to form through intensive weathering and erosion of the Hamersley landmass around 200 million years ago. Twenty million years ago, the Robe River valley was flooded by rising sea levels and iron-rich solutions leached from iron ore formations further inland and began to drain into the ancient Robe River system. These iron-rich solutions mixed with organic materials (eg, plant matter) and combined to form significant iron ore deposits along the Robe valley floor. Eventually, the sea retreated from the location of today's Pannawonica and further erosion and weathering of the Robe valley-floor left the harder pisolitic iron ore deposits to stand as mesas above the valley floor.[99]

The Beauty of Wildflower Season – Robe River Valley - Pannawonica

This photograph was taken on the side of one of the Robe River valley mesas. I had been fortunate to arrive in Pannawonica after unseasonal, and heavy, rain stimulated some of the best wildflower growth seen in the area for many years.

Pannawonica Hill in Wildflower Season – Robe River - Pannawonica

Depending upon which resource one looks to, the original Aboriginal name for Pannawonica Hill may have been one or more of three alternatives: different Aboriginal groups often had their own name for a landmark or location and often had their own stories as to how that landmark or location came into being.

The Department of Land Information records that Pannawonica Hill was originally referred to as "'Meedawandy' in the description of a lease" taken up by the Stewart family in February, 1878. The town telephone directory states that Aboriginal legend has it that Pannawonica Hill originally came from a place called Palaguni, and thereby took the same name.[103] Alternately, the book Some Ghosts, Some Not, quotes a local Aboriginal man as saying that Pannawonica Hill was once part of a Pilbara-coast island called Coolanboogan: that Pannawonica Hill did not originally have a name; and that Pannawonica Hill, was "stolen" in the dark of night by the devil people. The path that Pannawonica Hill cut while being "towed" now forms the bed of today's Robe River. According to this legend, the devil people lived around Pannawonica Hill and would climb to its peak to defend themselves against enemy attack. When the devil people passed on from that world they turned into a small red-chested bird with a white crown.[104]

Pannawonica Hill was discovered and named by surveyor, Frederick Brockman, in May, 1885.[105] While taking this photograph, a Brahman bull decided that I was not welcome. There were a few uneasy moments as I packed up my camera gear and made my way back to my vehicle as the bull moved directly toward me.

Millstream-Chichester National Park and the Chichester Range

Incorporating parts of the Chichester Range and the Fortesque River, the 200,000 hectare Millstream-Chichester National Park was formed by the amalgamation of the Millstream and Chichester Range National Parks in 1982. The area was first traversed by Francis Gregory in 1861 and it would appear that it was he that coined the name "Millstream" after "a fine tributary from the south, running strong enough to supply a large mill".[106]

Gregory also gave the name Chichester Downs after Chichester Fortesque, the Under Secretary of State for the Colonies, noting that "I have no doubt that at no distant period it will become a rich and thriving settlement."[107] Within four years, the area had been taken up as a grazing lease and, at its peak, the Millstream station covered more than 400,000 hectares and ran 55,000 sheep. The homestead now houses the visitor centre and was constructed in 1919.[108]

A Myriad of Pastel – Fortesque River – Chichester Range

I was fortunate to be directed to this most beautiful spot during my August, 2005 visit to Millstream and spent two nights searching for a photo that might accord it justice. The colours here were stunning; particularly, on sunset. This area would appear to have first been traversed by Gregory on 4 June, 1861. His diary notes: "White sandstone and shales began to make their appearance on the banks, and the water in the river had a saline taste."[112]

The area around Millstream itself consists of a series of five deep pools (Chinderwarriner, Deep Reach, Crossing, Livistona, and Palm), fed by springs discharging from the Millstream Aquifer. The Millstream Aquifer is saucer-shaped and occupies the buried valley of a large ancient river; the ancestor of today's Fortesque River. It covers an area of more than 2,000 square kilometres and, at Millstream, overflows; generally into the side of the Fortesque River bed (though one of the largest springs lies about 2.4 kilometres to the south and feeds the swift flowing Mill Stream itself. This runs north into the Fortesque River).[109]

Fern Detail – Mill Stream – Millstream-Chichester National Park

Millstream was first gazetted as a reserve in 1956 to stop its giant Melaleucas being cut for timber, although it did not include any of the deep pools in the Fortesque River or the springs which supplied them. The area was converted to a National Park in 1961. Until the construction of the Harding Dam in 1986, the Millstream Aquifer was the primary water source for the nearby towns of Karratha, Wickham, Dampier and Cape Lambert.[113]

Spinifex Aglow – Crossing Pool –
Millstream-Chichester National Park

Millstream's giant Melaleucas are generally found where
groundwater levels are within two metres of the ground surface.
Rivergums are generally found where groundwater levels are
within three metres of the ground surface. Recharge of the
Millstream Aquifer occurs by a combination of: (a) infiltration
from flood flows, where the Fortesque River crosses the aquifer
upstream of Deep Reach Pool; (b) direct infiltration of rainwater;
and, (c) by infiltration of small ephemeral creeks draining the
northern flank of the Hamersley Range. Average monthly
evaporation at Millstream ranges from 150mm in June to 400mm
in December.[114]

Blessed Reflections – Palm Pool – Millstream-Chichester National Park

This photograph came after a four kilometre paddle to the end of Palm Pool and back. A thick band of cloud moved in and it appeared certain that there would be no chance for a photo. Notwithstanding, I pulled the camera out just in case, and, battling mosquitos, we were rewarded with a 30 second sunlight window and this stunning vista. It pays never to give up: no matter how unlikely the situation appears. The name "Palm Pool" was recorded by Ian Elliot of the Department of Lands and Surveys from ranger Terry Hales of the Millstream-Chichester National Park on 9 June, 1983.[115]

Morning Light – Gregory Gorge – Chichester Range

Located outside Millstream-Chichester National Park, the rough approach to Gregory Gorge incorporates some of the most vibrant colour and unusual rock formations that I have seen. Gregory Gorge was discovered by Francis Gregory on 5 June, 1861.[116]

What makes Millstream so significant is that it incorporates a rare body of permanent water in a region characterised generally by dry stony hills and tablelands drained by intermittent rivers. This has stimulated the development of a different flora and fauna mix to other places in the Pilbara. The Millstream area incorporates the greatest diversity of bird species found anywhere in the Pilbara.[110] The Millstream Palm, with the exception of a small colony at Duck Creek on the Ashburton River, and a number of fern species are endemic to Millstream. Though the Hamersley Range has permanent water also, a different flora mix has evolved. There, many of the deep gorges have favoured the growth of plants requiring permanent shade.

Higher than it Looks – Pyramid Hill – Chichester Range

This photograph was taken on my second climb to the top of Pyramid Hill. On the first occasion, I had underestimated its height and arrived at the top a couple of minutes too late. On the way down, I slipped on the slope's steep and prevalent scree and took the back end out of my shorts. The views from the top are stunning, though the climb can be challenging.

Notwithstanding the unique habitat at Millstream, the Fortesque River system is in a constant and dynamic state of change. After the flood that accompanied Cyclone Joan in 1975, there was a change in flow from one of the pools that resulted in the widespread death of a large number of Melaleucas. Sediment accumulation also stopped the flow along a distributary channel that had previously discharged into a small pool, causing the pool to dry out. This had previously afforded an important waterbird habitat. [33]

Wildflower Season – Pyramid Hill – Chichester Range

As alluded to earlier, 2005 produced some of the best wildflower growth seen in the Pilbara for many years. The country around Karratha was covered with carpets of Mulla Mulla, Sturt's Desert Pea and an assortment of flowers incorporating yellows, whites, pinks and purples. This photograph was taken near the base of Pyramid Hill. The red/ black rock seen in the middle of the frame is basalt: a volcanic rock that was deposited as lava. Naturally of dark green to grey colour, this rock weathers over much of the Chichester Range to a red, clay-rich, soil called Gilgai. [117]

Morning Reflections – George River – Millstream-Chichester National Park

This walk was one of the more difficult that I have undertaken in recent times. With about 20 kilos of gear on my back – 15 of those being camera gear – I pushed up-river for about 12 to 13 kilometres. Boulders and thick paperbarks blocked my path for much of the way. The physical and mental effort that it took to remove my pack and walk the 20 metres to take this photo was enormous. I returned to my vehicle on the following day, dehydrated – despite consuming about seven litres of water – and physically and mentally spent. One of my camera lenses took a jolt during the return journey compromising some subsequent, and what had been time-consuming and expensive photographs.

Wittenoom

Wittenoom proved to be one of the more intriguing of the Pilbara towns that I visited. Were it not for the urgings of my girlfriend, Fiona, and for the prompting of a Tom Price GP, it would probably not have been covered in this book. Wittenoom was named after Frank Wittenoom, with George Hancock, a partner in nearby Mulga Downs Station. The mining of blue asbestos (crocidolite) was its raison d'etre – an activity that had commenced in nearby Wittenoom Gorge in 1938. However, it was not until 1947 that construction of a town had commenced.[118] The town was formally gazetted on 5 May, 1950[119], and by the end of 1966, the Hamersley Range and Wittenoom Gorge had produced 15,246,694 tonnes of blue asbestos. This made it Western Australia's fourth most valuable commodity after gold, coal and iron ore. At its peak, Wittenoom was home to 1,500 people and was the largest inland town in Western Australia's north.[120]

The decline of Wittenoom was equally rapid. High production costs and limited ore reserves saw the mine close on 31 December, 1966 and, in the last month of mining, at least one family departed the town daily. What remained of the town's population – around 100 – moved to capitalise on the town's proximity to the stunningly beautiful gorges of the Hamersley Range and, by the end of the 1960s, the town had again grown in size to around 500. In 1979, the State moved to close the town down; ostensibly on the back of allegations that airborne blue asbestos fibres exist over the town in unsafe quantities. This has led to a "standoff" between residents determined to stay and a Government determined to get them out.[121]

Mario Hartmann - Old Catholic Church and Fire Truck - Wittenoom.

I met Mario during a 2005 visit to Wittenoom. Originally from Austria, Mario first visited the town in 1987 and "liked it". He now owns a part share in the Wittenoom Guesthouse (a converted convent) and runs the town powerhouse. Three times a week he carries out the "mail-run" to Auski Roadhouse, some 42 kilometres to the town's east.

Analysis of the argument put forward by Government as justification for Wittenoom's closure is interesting and revealing. It argues that the town's proximity to the old Wittenoom Gorge tailings dump - about 10 kilometres – exposes its residents to an unacceptably high risk of asbestos-related death. Residents of Wittenoom however question why, if proximity to tailings is such a problem, that nearby Karijini National Park is promoted so heavily. Oxer's Lookout, Weano, Knox and Hancock Gorges all lie about five kilometres to the south-east of the tailings dump: a major problem (one would think) when the dominant winds during the peak of the tourist season (June, July and August) are easterlies.[122]

Wittenoom residents believe rather that the Government determination to remove their town involves something more simple: specifically that high grade mineral deposits have been identified nearby. On this basis, they argue, the townsite lies directly in the path of what could be a rail-line linking deposits to the east with major railway systems to the town's west. Why a rail line could not bypass the town stems from the fact that the country north of the town is part of the Fortesque River floodplain. Furthermore, they question why, if Wittenoom Gorge is so unsafe, Government-appointed contractors continue to use the gorge as a water re-stocking point.[123]

Royal Mulla Mulla (*Ptilotus rotundifolius*) – Wittenoom Gorge. Perhaps my favourite wildflower, the Royal Mulla Mulla tends not to be anywhere near as common as the Tall Mulla Mulla (*Ptilotus exaltatus*). In 2005, unseasonal July rains produced some of the most stunning wildflower growth seen in the area for many years. I was astonished to see blankets of Royal Mulla Mulla at various places throughout the Hamersley Range: something I had not seen before.

The Central Pilbara Coast and Surrounds

Roebourne[124]

Roebourne owes its foundation to the 1861 explorations of Francis Gregory and to the subsequent settlement of the area by his cousin, Emma Withnell, and her husband, John. Encouraged by Gregory's reports of favourable pastoral country, John and Emma Withnell left Fremantle for Tien Tsin Harbour (now Cossack) on the *Sea Ripple* in March, 1864. They were accompanied by their two young sons, George and John, several other family members and by three servants.

Near Mangrove Harbour (now Port Hedland), the *Sea Ripple* encountered bad weather and struck a reef, causing it to list badly. Over the ensuing days, most of the horses, cattle and 650 ewes perished and the party suffered badly as repairs were effected to their distressed vessel. When the party finally arrived at Tien Tsin Harbour on 14 April, 1864, they established camp and John Withnell pushed up-river to find a more suitable location for settlement, eventually choosing a site at the base of a small hill overlooking a large freshwater pool.

On arriving at Tien Tsin Harbour, Emma Withnell became the first European woman to settle in the north-west[125] and named the hill overlooking their new home, Mt Welcome[126], on the basis that "[i]t gave us shelter and rest at the end of our long journey". The settlement became known as the Harding River settlement and established itself quickly as the social and administrative centre of the Pilbara. On 17 August, 1866, the settlement became the first town to be gazetted in the North-West. It was named Roebourne, in honour of the State's first Surveyor-General, John Septimus Roe.

Prior to 1984, the Roebourne gaol was used as the State's primary facility for the housing of medium and long-term Aboriginal prisoners. During the 1870s, the State enacted legislation that mandated the provision of minimum conditions relating to food, clothing and health for Aboriginal employees. Aboriginal employees were required, as part of their contract with their employer, to remain with their employer. Any failure to do so would attract three months imprisonment. It was intended that the legislation would allay the concerns of some about the treatment of many Indigenous workers. At the same time it would ensure station access to the cheap labour force on which they were then so dependent.

Local artist Christine Willis stands in front of the old Roebourne "lock-up". Designed by government architect, George Temple Poole, the gaol, police and courthouse precinct was unique for the fact that it incorporated three disparate law enforcement elements within one area. Despite the good intentions of the legislation, it was unfortunate that the police station, gaol and courthouse ended up dealing more with the significant numbers of Aboriginal people that broke their contracts. Pastoralists were more often fined for breach of their obligations and these fines were either not enforced or not heeded.

Cossack

Originally called Tien Tsin, after the privately chartered sheep carrying barque which landed there in April 1863, Cossack was gazetted as a town, and as the port for Roebourne, on 24 May, 1872.[127] It was the first port to be established in the North-West and between 1863 and the 1890s provided a vital point of access for the settlement and development of the Pilbara region. It was renamed Cossack by Governor Weld in 1871, after the ship in which he had visited the district. To the time of its sudden decline in the late 1890s, it held an interdependent relationship with nearby Roebourne. Roebourne, which was then the administrative centre for the north of the colony, depended upon the harbour facilities and services at Cossack, while Cossack depended upon Roebourne for its supplies of freshwater.[128]

To the 1890s Cossack was a major staging point for the North-West pearling fleet. This led to a major influx of Asian and Aboriginal labourers. It also acted as a departure point for prospectors destined for the Pilbara and Kimberley goldfields, and then later, the Murchison and Ashburton fields. During this time, its population grew to around 3,000 people. Pearling – with its high mortality rates and poor pay and living conditions – struggled to attract white Australians. Cossack grew to accommodate different communities outside of the main residential area of European settlers: a "Chinatown", a "Malaytown" and a "Japtown".[129]

The decline of Cossack during the late 1890s was equally as rapid. This was in part due to the relocation of the pearling fleet to Broome, the consistent silting up of the port and the relocation of shipping to Port Hedland that followed the discovery of gold at Marble Bar and Nullagine. While the buildings that remain today are of local bluestone construction, it is interesting to note that, up to 1888, all the buildings in Cossack were originally of wooden construction. Those with galvanised iron roofs were anchored down with steel cables attached to cement blocks embedded in the ground.[130]

The mouth of the Harding River, at which Cossack is located, is significant for the fact that all known varieties of mangrove in Western Australia are represented within close proximity.[131]

Wickham and Cape Lambert

Located 15 kilometres from Karratha, the town of Wickham was constructed to house the majority of people working at Cape Lambert; the port built to service the Robe River iron ore project. Construction of Wickham commenced in 1970, and, though its design was predicated on an eventual population of 12,000 people, the population peaked at 5,000 in 1978-9. Wickham was declared as a town on 26 November, 1971 and was named after Captain John Wickham who had surveyed the North-West coast in the *HMS Beagle* between 1838 and 1840. Cape Lambert was named by Commander Philip Parker King on 5 March, 1818 in compliment to his friend Aylmer Bourke Lambert.[132]

A key factor in the viability of the Robe project was the port design proposed by the successful tenderer, Clough. Their bid, at A$13M, was around a third of that of the next nearest tender and utilised A-frame steel piles rather than more traditional heavy structures. The Dutch designers considered that this design would offer less resistance to ocean forces and would ultimately prove more stable. A longer jetty length (2.6 kilometres) was preferred as it was considered that the additional up-front costs would be more than offset by the higher dredging costs that would be necessary if a shorter jetty was constructed. And, in settling upon a jetty height some 18.9 metres above high-water mark (the structure from sea-bed to deck is some 40 metres), annual cyclonic activity was a major consideration. It would now take a wave of sufficient height to break over the upper floor of the Victoria Hotel in Roebourne, about 15 kilometres inland, to break over the jetty's decking.[133]

The ore wharf at Cape Lambert is 444 metres long and is reached by a 2.3 kilometre long finger pier which supports two 1.5 metre wide conveyors and a lane light roadway. The largest vessel to have berthed at the wharf was 323,000 Dead Weight Tonnes ("DWT"). [135] The port has three berths. Two ship loaders enable up to two vessels to be loaded simultaneously and studies are underway for expansion of the port beyond its current 55 – 57 million tonne annual capacity. [136]

Point Samson and Port Walcott[136]

Point Samson was named after Michael Samson, a member of a prominent Fremantle family, and second officer of the *Tien Tsin*, during Walter Padbury's expedition to Nickol Bay in 1863. It was declared a town during 1902, though it was not gazetted until 2 July, 1909, when the misspelt name, Point *Sampson,* was recorded. The official misspelling persisted for some years when it was re-gazetted as Point Samson on 10 April, 1918.[137]

As a result of silting problems at the nearby port of Cossack, and the need to accommodate visits of larger vessels to the area, a deep-water port was established at Port Walcott around 1903. When this jetty was destroyed by a cyclone in 1925, Cossack enjoyed a brief re-emergence as the region's service port until a new jetty was completed at Port Walcott in 1935. Cyclone Orson inflicted severe damage to the jetty in 1989 and it was removed, as a result, in 1991.

Prior to completion of the Cliffs Robe River facility at Cape Lambert, and the Hamersley Iron facility at Dampier, Port Walcott enjoyed an active and, at times, booming history. Port movements included copper, livestock, wood, pearl-shell, kangaroo skin, and bagged asbestos from the one-time boom-town of Wittenoom. The commissioning of the Tom Price and Robe River iron-ore projects in the late 1960s and early 1970s saw the port used extensively to unload major infrastructure materials. When these projects were completed, Point Samson and its port lost their primary income source. The last ship to leave the port was the *Kangaroo* in 1976.

Honeymoon Cove – Point Samson. The origin of this name can be traced back to the 1930s when the Country Women's Association rented a seaside cottage at Point Samson. The cottage was well utilised by people from surrounding pastoral stations and it would appear that newly-weds delighted in swimming there.[138]

Karratha

Gazetted as a town on 8 August, 1969, Karratha owes its existence to the expansion of the Hamersley Iron Project, the desire of the State to establish a regional administrative centre and the commencement of construction of the Dampier Salt Project in 1968. Prior to the town's gazettal, Hamersley Iron had accommodated staff in the "company-owned" town of Dampier. However, the rugged topography of the surrounding terrain there prevented further expansion. Development of Karratha was undertaken jointly by the State and Hamersley Iron as an open town. Both sides contributed to its capital infrastructure needs. The first occupants of the new town moved into their homes on June 28 and 29, 1970.[139]

Karratha is now a thriving regional town of around 11,000[140] people. Citing REIWA data, Brady First National Real Estate noted a median residential price increase during the financial year of nearly 12%. Growth has been driven by surrounding resource projects (eg, the North-West Shelf Gas Project) and associated developments such as the A$630M Burrup Fertilisers Ammonium Plant. The North-West Shelf Gas Project led to a doubling of the town's population in the space of 10 years. In the late 1980s, it was the world's largest natural resource project. The dollars of the day cost of the project, by the time of its completion in the mid 1990s, was in the vicinity of A$12B: substantially larger than the inflation adjusted cost of A$4B – A$7B for the Snowy Mountains Scheme, which up to that time had held the mantle for Australia's largest engineering undertaking.[141]

Folded Rock Strata – Cleaverville Beach – Karratha. Karratha is located on the shores of Nickol Bay and takes its name from the Karratha Station pastoral lease, within whose boundaries it was once located. The name Karratha is taken from an Aboriginal word meaning "good country" or "soft earth" and was accorded to Karratha Station by its first owners, Dr Baynton and Harry Whittal-Venn. Nickol Bay was named by Lieutenant Philip Parker King on March 4, 1818 during his explorations of the Australian coast.[142] Francis Gregory subsequently used it as the base from which he launched his 1861 explorations of the region.

Dampier

Gazetted as a town on 30 June, 1972[143], the town of Dampier, and its accompanying port, were constructed to service the iron ore mine at Tom Price, 288 kilometres to the south-east. Construction of both facilities commenced in 1965. The first ore shipment took place on 16 August, 1966 when the *Tachikawa Maru* sailed with 20,000 tonnes of lump ore for Japan. By 1979, Hamersley Iron had shipped more than 300 million tonnes of ore in some 4,000 ships.[144]

Since the initial completion of the general cargo and Parker Point wharves, these have been continually upgraded. The Parker Point ore wharf today accepts vessels up to a nominal 180,000 DWT and a wharf at East Intercourse Island has accepted vessels up to 320,000 DWT.

In 1972, Dampier Salt commenced salt operations via the use of solar evaporation in nearby crystallisation ponds[145] and in the year ended 30 June, 2005 some 2.9 million tonnes of salt left the port on 81 ships.[146] The bulk of this product is destined for the global petrochemical industry. In 1980, Woodside Offshore Petroleum and its joint venture partners chose Dampier as the site for the onshore Liquified Natural Gas ("LNG") production plant and export wharf. The North Rankin A production platform was constructed 130 kilometres north-north-west of Dampier and connected by pipeline to the onshore site at Withnell Bay. This was followed by construction of a second jetty in the last quarter of 1995; one designed to accept both Liquified Petroleum Gas ("LPG") vessels and condensate tankers.

It was against the above background that the story of "Red Dog" developed. Born "Tally Ho" at Paraburdoo in 1971, Red Dog moved with his family to Dampier when he was about 18 months old. He broke ties with his family shortly after and became a wanderer. He eventually befriended one of the bus drivers in the Hamersley Iron Transport section and soon began to ride the Hamersley Iron buses between Karratha and Dampier. He travelled on courier vehicles and trucks and he would regularly travel the 288 kilometres between Dampier and Tom Price on the Hamersley Iron train. He also travelled to Roebourne, Point Samson, Port Hedland, Broome and to Perth (on at least two occasions) though he would always reappear in Dampier or Karratha. Often, on recognising a vehicle or driver, he would jump out in front of the moving vehicle to force it to stop. He would only disembark when he reached the location to which he wished to go: even if it necessitated that the driver go some distance out of his or her way. Red Dog died after apparently taking a strychnine bait in Karratha on 10 November, 1979. His death was reported across the State and a Memorial Fund was launched on 30 November, 1979.[147]

Dampier retains the record for the largest cargo ever loaded at an Australian port. 261,391 tonnes of iron ore left for Japan on the *Grand Phoenix* in November, 1995.[148] Work on the Tom Price railway was undertaken in parallel with the port and involved the laying of 648,000 jarrah and wandoo sleepers (each weighing 100 kilograms) and 38,000 tonnes of rail in less than 12 months.[149] At the time of this book going to print, some A$20 – A$24B worth of projects were earmarked in the vicinity of Dampier.[150]

North-West Shelf Gas Project[151]

The North-West Shelf Natural Gas Project owes its foundation to the discovery of natural gas at Scott Reef No.1 in 1971 by a consortium led by Woodside (Lakes Entrance) Oil NL. Woodside was listed in 1954 during the share market boom that followed the discovery of oil at Rough Range near Exmouth in 1953. It was established to search for oil in the Gippsland region of south-east Victoria but was ultimately unsuccessful. Around 1962, Woodside began to consider Western Australia's North-West Shelf. Its chief geologist, Dr Nicholas Boutakoff, had noted that there were vast unexplored sedimentary basins between the Bonaparte Gulf (in the north Kimberley) and Barrow Island (to the west of Karratha). Woodside moved quickly and, in 1963, applied for 367,000 square kilometres of permits covering the entire North-West Shelf: the only part of that area not, to that time, held by West Australian Petroleum Pty Ltd ("WAPET").

Within ten years of the exploration permits having been granted, Woodside had assembled a consortium that was conducting Australia's largest ever exploration programme. The first well was drilled at Ashmore Reef in 1967 (north-west of Broome) and was followed by a further 10 wells, before a substantial gas/ condensate discovery was made at Scott Reef in 1971, off the Broome coast. Though Scott Reef was uncommercial, as a result of it being 430 kilometres from the coast, "pay-dirt" was struck weeks later with the discovery of a major gas/ condensate field at North Rankin. This discovery was much closer to the Pilbara coast and, by early 1972,

two other large prospects in the same region had been identified (Angel and Goodwyn). The three fields were grouped about 130 kilometres off the Pilbara coast at depths of between 90 and 130 metres.

On August 24, 1977, the North-West Shelf Natural Gas Project was formally approved by the Commonwealth and West Australian governments. The first step involved the supply of natural gas to the Perth-based State Electricity Commission of Western Australia ("SECWA") via pipeline that routed through Dampier. Gas destined for the local market would also be used to supply the Pilbara iron-ore province. An offshore production platform was constructed at North Rankin and commenced production in 1984. The second stage of the project involved the supply of LNG to eight Japanese gas and electricity utilities. A second platform was constructed in 1986 on the same field to serve the export markets. By the early 1990s, a third platform was established on the Goodwyn field. A pipeline from offshore was constructed to link with a gas treatment plant at Withnell Bay. This now produces sales gas, LNG, condensate and LPG. A supply base and shipping facilities were established near the site of the Dampier Port Authority.

Woodside produces around 600,000 barrels of oil equivalent per day and plans to increase this to one million barrels per day by 2007. It is projected that, by 2007-8, production will come from five LNG trains, five floating production storage and off-take vessels, five offshore platforms and an onshore gas and condensate operation.[152]

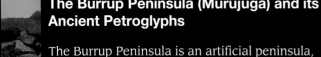

The Burrup Peninsula (Murujuga) and its Ancient Petroglyphs

The Burrup Peninsula is an artificial peninsula, connected to the mainland by a causeway that was created during the 1960s. The service causeway supports both road and rail-track and incorporates levee banks to prevent tidal inundation. Following construction of the causeway, its name was changed from Dampier Island to Dampier Peninsula. In 1978, Woodside requested that its name be changed to the Burrup Peninsula, after the name of the highest mountain on the Peninsula. This was to avoid confusion with the Dampier Peninsula to the north of Broome. Mt Burrup was named after Henry Burrup, a bank clerk who was murdered in Roebourne on 13 January, 1885. Though different Aboriginal groups may have different names for the Burrup, collectively they refer to it as Murujuga, meaning 'hip bone sticking out'.[153]

The Burrup Peninsula is home to what might well be the world's most extensive, diverse and concentrated collection of rock inscriptions (petroglyphs). They are of obvious cultural and aesthetic importance and are significant for their quantum. Estimates suggest that there could be substantially more than 10,000 petroglyphs on the Burrup.[154] They have archaeological and natural history import and document the diets, lifestyle and evolution of an ancient culture. Some have suggested that Burrup petroglyphs could be as old as 18,500 years;[155] others

because the petroglyphs incorporate a strong emphasis on marine fauna, marine exploitation (and hence inscription of the petroglyphs) is likely to have occurred when sea levels stabilised at the end of the last Ice Age some 7,000 years ago.[156]

At a cultural level, local Aboriginal peoples believe the rock inscriptions to be permanent signs left by ancestral beings, during the Dreaming, when the earth was soft. These ancestral beings are believed to have formulated rules of social conduct for human beings to follow. The rock inscriptions remain as evidence of their existence, and as a permanent visual reminder of the Law they formulated. These sites were also places of continuing spiritual power and some sites were associated with rituals or totemic ceremonies.

In February 1868, members of the Yaburara tribe are alleged to have stolen flour from a pearling boat anchored in Nickol Bay. According to official account, a policeman and his Aboriginal assistant arrested a suspect and camped near the coast, a few kilometres west of the Nickol River mouth. During the night, other Aborigines freed the suspect, who had been chained to a tree. They speared the policeman and his assistant and two white pearlers. Two parties of special constables were sent to apprehend the villains who, by then, had fled to the islands around Flying Foam Passage. Over the next few days the special constables roamed the islands around Flying Foam Passage, firing upon any Aborigines they saw.

The Dampier Climbing Man Site. This site is one of the most outstanding small rock-art complexes on the Burrup Peninsula: for its cultural and historical importance and for its aesthetic values.[161] It is world-famous and we were fortunate to be shown what is a Protected Site by Shane Peterson of Burrup Peninsula Rock Art Tours. The tours are excellent and Shane has tremendous knowledge of the Aboriginal and European history in the area. He can be contacted on 0402 364 861.

Though the special constable reported killing five to ten Aborigines, other estimates range from 30 to what is thought to be an exaggerated figure of 150. The killings became known as the "Flying Foam Massacre", and brought an end to the Yaburara as a cohesive social unit. The Burrup petroglyphs therefore document the last vestiges of an extinct group of people.[157]

Though the Yaburara have passed on, new challenges exist for today's custodians of the Burrup petroglyphs. Industry on the Burrup is worth billions of dollars to the Australian economy. However, the prevalence and concentration of petroglyphs has already lead to competition for space and the relocation of some inscriptions from their original location (eg, at Hearson Cove): a concern given the importance of context in ascribing meaning. Opponents to further development argue that the importance of the Burrup petroglyphs lies not just in their historical import, but in the fact that they offer Aboriginal people a way forward by leveraging tourism and hence, employment. It will be an enormous test for policy-makers to marry what, on the surface, appear to be conflicting objectives.

Geologically, the Burrup Peninsula is comprised mostly of a fine-grained granite and gabbro that "intruded as a sill of magma between layers of surrounding volcanic and sedimentary rocks".[158] The sill is thought to be at least two kilometres thick and formed around 2.7 billion years ago.[159] Hearson Cove was named by Francis Gregory on 16 May, 1861 after the second mate of the barque, the *Dolphin*, who was injured when a gun, carried by a fellow crew-member, accidentally discharged.[160]

Dampier Archipelago[162]

The Dampier Archipelago consists of 42 islands, islets and rocks lying within a 45 kilometre radius of Dampier. While it was named by Nicolas Baudin, during his 1801 voyage in the *Geographe* along the Western Australian coast, it appears that the Archipelago was known to Dutch navigators at least as early as 1628. Then, it appeared with Barrow and Montebello Islands on a chart drawn for the Dutch East India Company. In 1699, William Dampier, in his vessel, the *Roebuck*, landed at an island that he named Rosemary Island. However, this naming appears to have been misinterpreted by Baudin and he renamed the island Malus Island. The name Rosemary was assigned to an island four kilometres to the north-west. Baudin also named Legendre, Hauy and Delambre Islands during his visit.

Early Morning in the vicinity of Gidley Island.

At least eight species of marine mammal occur in the waters of the Dampier Archipelago. These include: the Dugong, which use the shallow bays and areas between the islands for feeding on sea grasses; the Humpback Whale; three species of dolphin; the False Killer Whale; and, the Southern Bottle-nosed Dolphin. Four species of marine turtle, including the Green, Hawksbill, Flatback and Loggerhead, use island beaches for nesting during the warmer Wet-season months.

The Dampier Archipelago, like the Buccaneer and Bonaparte Archipelagos off the Kimberley coast, was created by rising sea levels brought about by the end of the last Ice Age, that commenced around 18,000 years ago. Then, it is thought that sea levels rose by around 180 metres over a period of 11,000 years (about 1.5 centimetres annually) and the coast retreated inland by between 180 and 200 kilometres (or 15 metres annually). There is no permanent freshwater known on the islands, though freshwater is available for part of the year from rock pools following rain. Islands range in size from one-hectare rock islets to the 3,290 hectare Enderby Island. The oldest rock types, found at Dolphin, Tozer and Enderby Islands, are granites and granite gneiss. They exceed 2.8 billion years in age.

Sunrise above Gidley Island.

102 species of bird have been recorded in the Archipelago, including 16 species of sea-bird and 10 shorebird species and there are a number of important nesting sites. Forty-one species of land-based reptile are known, including the King Brown. The Death Adder has not been found, though it has been sighted on the Burrup Peninsula and there is a possibility that it might also be found in the Archipelago in time.

With Cossack's development as a major pearling centre in the early 1870s, the Dampier Archipelago was fished extensively for pearl shell. Remains of a pearling camp are evident at Black Hawke Bay on Gidley Island. Between 1870 and 1872, a whaling station was established at Malus Island to process Humpback whales taken by long boats throughout the Archipelago. Remains of this station may still be found. Between 1900 and 1963, turtles and eggs were taken commercially in the area, before large tides made the Archipelago's shallow waters too dirty to catch profitably. A turtle-meat canning company was located at Cossack until 1936.

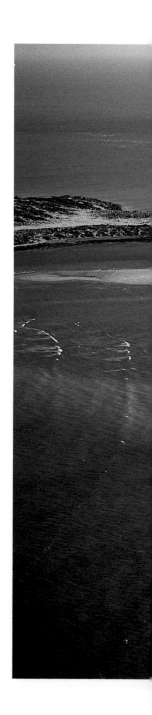

Colours of the Dampier Archipelago.

Like the Bonaparte and Buccaneer Archipelagos off the Kimberley coast, and unlike the mainland, the Dampier Archipelago is significant for its native flora and fauna populations. These have remained largely unaffected by the impact of fire and exotic species (eg, feral cats and foxes) brought about by the arrival of European man.

The Perentie *(Varanus giganteus)* - Near Carawine Gorge - Marble Bar.

The scientific name of the Perentie means giant monitor. The Perentie grows up to 2.5 metres in length and is Australia's largest monitor lizard. It is found in Australia's arid regions and feeds on snakes, lizards, birds and small mammals. This photograph was taken near Carawine Gorge in the East Pilbara from a distance of about 1.5 metres.

The Osprey *(Pandion haliaetus)* -West Lewis Island - Dampier Archipelago.

Ospreys feed on fish and are found throughout the world, with the exception of Antarctica. They have a wingspan of 1.5 metres and lay up to three eggs which take around 37 days to hatch. Fledgling of the young, like this one here, takes seven to eight weeks.

The Town of Onslow[163]

Located near the mouth of the Ashburton River, Onslow owes its foundation largely to the pioneering efforts of James Clark and John McKenzie. Clark had been chief engineer on the sailing ship, *Rob Roy* when, in 1882, the ship became stranded in a tidal creek during a fierce storm. During the resulting land journey home, Clark was encouraged to consider the establishment of a business in the area. Local pastoralists were having difficulty transporting their wool to Fremantle for sale as there were no service or supply facilities in the area.

On reaching Fremantle, Clark linked with his brother-in-law, McKenzie, and the two purchased a 21-ton ketch, which they named the *Ashburton*. They left Fremantle on 11 August, 1883 and arrived at the mouth of the Ashburton River on 23 August, 1883. Here, they were soon required to deal with the effects of a tidal wave, triggered by the eruption of the giant Indonesian volcano, Krakatoa. Despite losing much of their cargo before they could unload, they established camp near the area's only freshwater source. This became the site of what is now known as "Old Onslow". This site was gazetted as the town of Onslow on 26 October, 1885. Silting problems at the mouth of the Ashburton necessitated a move to the site of the current town in the early 1920s.

Mulla Mulla season amidst the termite mounds. Related to cockroaches, not ants, termites are herbivores that convert the nutrients from grass and wood into protein. Termite mounds are created by termites cementing grains of soil together with saliva and excreta. They typically contain numerous galleries, along which the termites move. A royal chamber and nursery exists at their centre and it is here that the Queen of the species is found. Australia is home to about 350 of the estimated 2,300 termite species globally.[166] Here, I was prompted to stop the vehicle by my girlfriend, Fiona, and was dazzled by the sunset-illuminated array of colour across the landscape. A local had said prior to our departure (it was late September, 2005) that the country looked better than it had done at any other time during the preceding 30 years.

Onslow was the southern-most town to be bombed by the Japanese during the Second World War, though it sustained no casualties. All attacks occurred during 1943 on nights of a full moon. In September, 1963, the North-West Coastal Highway was re-routed by the Main Roads Department. A sealed road now by-passed Onslow. On 25 September, 1986, a sealed access road of 82 kilometres was opened linking the town with the Highway. Nearby Nanutarra Roadhouse was built in 1965. Today, and like Nullagine in the far east of the region, Onslow could be about to experience significant expansion. In recent years, it has become the site of a major salt project – the Onslow Salt Project effected its first shipment on 28 July, 2001 – and BHP Billiton intends to install a major LNG processing plant as part of a new gas-field development.

Onslow takes its name from Sir Alexander Campbell Onslow, who was the Chief Justice and Acting Governor at the time Onslow was settled. Captain Philip Parker King would appear to have been the first European to sight the Ashburton River and named it the Curlew after the estuary's many birds. However, Gregory, during his 1861 explorations, on reaching the river and thinking it to be a different one to that sighted by King, named it the Ashburton after Lord Ashburton who was then President of the Royal Geographic Society. Some time later, Trevarton Sholl and H.W. Venn led a party inland. Realising that the Curlew and Ashburton were one and the same, he elected to keep the latter and so the Ashburton name was retained.

Wildflowers – near Mt Murray – Nanutarra.

Another "lucky" shot. I had spent some time photographing the wildflowers seen in the foreground of this photograph before I was called to attend to a matter in Port Hedland. On passing through Karratha, I collected some processed film and discovered a problem with one of the lenses that I had been using. As a result, the initial photographs were rendered unuseable. I returned a few days later and was fortunate to find that the wildflowers were still in-tact. I was able to re-shoot the scene and this image resulted.

Cattle and the Pilbara

Over the last 20 or so years, many Pilbara stations have chosen to convert from sheep to cattle. This has been driven largely by the collapse in the wool market, which, in turn, has stemmed from the increasing availability of cheaper synthetic textiles. In the 12 months to the end of 2004, it is estimated that total sheep numbers fell from 32,000 to 16,000. Cattle numbers increased, during the same period, from 113,000 to 170,000. At the end of 2004, there were 61 pastoral leases. Ten of these were held by Aboriginal interests and 10 by mining. Overall, there were 50 pastoral businesses from which virtually all of the herd turn-off went to Perth for domestic sale (unlike the Kimberley which relies heavily on the live export industry).[165]

Bos-indicus-type cattle have a number of characteristics that make them more able to withstand the hot, humid, climate of the tropics than their European counterparts. These include: (a) a short thick glossy goat that reflects many of the sun's rays and enables it to graze during the heat of the day; (b) more highly developed sweat glands and an ability to perspire more freely; (c) the production of an oily secretion in their skin that may help repel insects; (d) loose skin that increases the body surface area exposed to cooling; (e) the fact that they produce less internal body heat; and, (f) a large hump over the top of the shoulder and neck that is comprised of fat, gristle and beef and that serves as a reservoir (in the same way as the hump(s) of a camel) in times of limited feed and/or water.[166]

Dinnertime in the Stock Camp – Nanutarra Station.

This photograph was taken during two days that I spent on Nanutarra Station in September, 2005. The stock camp had a good feel to it and is perhaps one of the few "old-time" stock camps that exists today. Here, chopper pilots and ringers take a breather and a bite to eat after a morning's mustering and yard-work.

It is possible that overall herd genetics in the Pilbara may be better than those found in parts of the Kimberley. This stems from the fact that there tend to be fewer clean-skin short-horn bulls in parts of the Pilbara and there tends to be a greater infusion of bos-indicus genetics. The elimination of short-horn bulls in parts of the Pilbara has made it easier to infuse herds with bos-indicus-type genetics. Short-horn bulls compete with bos-indicus-type bulls and will nearly always dominate. In the Kimberley, the topography is more rugged and natural waters more common. There, clean-skin bulls exist in greater numbers because they have been able to penetrate into rocky country where it is difficult and cost-prohibitive to muster. The absence of fewer natural waters in the Pilbara means that cattle tend to congregate around man-made waters. This has made it easier to control the location of herds and eradicate cattle with inferior genetics (eg, clean-skin short-horn bulls).

In the yards – Nanutarra Station.

Cattle are fed and watered on completion of the day's mustering activities. Like many stations in the Pilbara, Nanutarra has converted across to a largely bos-indicus-type herd to meet the preferences of domestic and international markets and which is more climate-suitable.

Exmouth

European activity in the Exmouth region dates back to 1618, when Captain Jacobsz, in the *Mauritius*, landed at North-West Cape. However, the foundation for Exmouth, as it exists today, was not laid until 1962, when North-West Cape was chosen as the site for a US Navy communication station. The base was set up to supply communications to submarines and ships patrolling the south-west Pacific and Indian Oceans. Its construction saw the area's population increase from 41 in 1961 to 2,248 in 1966. The Base's Very Low Frequency ("VLF") towers were, at the time of their completion in 1967, the highest manmade structures in the southern hemisphere. Until the transfer of control of the station to the Australian Defence Forces in 1992, Exmouth was characterised by a sizeable US expatriate population.[167]

Prior to the construction of the communication station, the handful of people that inhabited the North-West Cape were essentially reliant on the pastoral, fishing and prawning industries. In 1942, the fall of the Philippines to the Japanese saw the establishment of an Allied Forces base at the Bay of Rest (called Operation Potshot). This had the purpose of refuelling north-bound submarines and acted as a staging point for reconnaissance seaplanes. The scheme proved to be unsuccessful and, after Japanese bombing raids in 1943, the base was wound-down. It was ultimately abandoned in 1945.[168]

Construction of Vlamingh Head Lighthouse commenced in 1911 as a result of a number of shipwrecks that occurred on the reef nearby: for example, the wreck of the *SS Mildura* which occurred in 1907 without human casualty. The lighthouse became operational on 10 November, 1912. Two lighthouse keepers were employed for the maintenance and running of the kerosene-fuelled warning beacon. This was visible for up to 22 nautical miles. Their stores, given the fact that the town of Exmouth was not actually gazetted until 1963, arrived by ship and were brought to the lighthouse via a 6.5 kilometre horse-drawn cart trip. In 1967, the lighthouse was decommissioned. This coincided with the official opening of the US Naval Communication Base at nearby North-West Cape in the same year. One of the high VLF towers now fulfils the former role of the lighthouse.

Vlamingh Lighthouse – North-West Cape

Exmouth Gulf was named by Captain Philip Parker King on February 18, 1818 "in compliment to the noble and gallant Viscount" [Sir Edward Pellew, Viscount of Exmouth].[169] King also named North-West Cape after the direction in which it lies.[170] "The fall of the high-land was called Vlamingh Head, after the navigator [William de Vlamingh] who first discovered this part."[171]

Dune Detail - Jurabi Coastal Park.

I have a fascination with untouched sand dunes and the unique
patterns that can sometimes be found. This was taken during the
middle of the day while returning from a shoot at Turquoise Bay
and Trealla Beach.

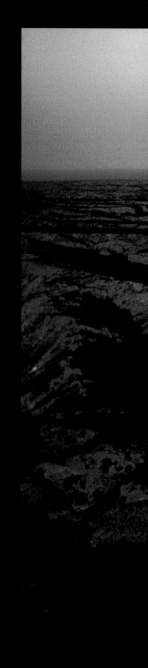

Cape Range National Park

Located near Exmouth, the 50,580 hectare[172] Cape Range National Park was a real photographic challenge. My first visit yielded no photos that I felt portrayed the essence of the landscape. The bold contrasting colours that I like to chase, and the existence of major stand-out features, tend not to be as obvious when viewed at ground-level. On my return, I took to the skies. Seen from the air, particularly in the hour after sunrise, Cape Range National Park, with its contrast of pastel and shadow, is truly spectacular. This is by far the best way to see Cape Range: particularly for someone with limited time. Norwest Airwork Aerial Tours, with whom I flew, have operations at Exmouth, Yardie, Coral Bay and Onslow. I could not recommend them highly enough for any air charter. They can be contacted on (08) 9949 2888.

Shadows and Contours – Charles Knife Canyon.

The western escarpment of Cape Range is characterised by a series of fossilised coral reefs that provide evidence of the various Ice-Age sea levels and a record of the marine animals that so inhabited them. Where the original limestone is exposed on the upper ridges, fossilised teeth of giant sharks can be seen.

The Charles Knife Canyon Road was constructed to facilitate access for WAPET drilling teams searching for oil. It took four months to build and was, at the time of its construction, regarded as a major engineering feat, due to the many steep inclines that had to be renegotiated. It takes its name from the person who surveyed its path (and who, incidentally, was not a qualified surveyor or engineer).[173]

Cape Range National Park is significant for the fact that it contains more plant species – there are over 630 species of vascular plants representing, unusually, all three of Western Australia's botanical provinces – than any other semi-arid or limestone karst area in Western Australia.[173] Together with provinces in the Kimberley and Nullabor Plain, it is one of only three major limestone areas in Western Australia. The fact that it has been cut from the mainland, at various times, by higher sea levels than those existing now, has enabled the evolution of unique species of flora and fauna.[174]

Range to Reef – Cape Range National Park.

The cave gudgeon and cave eel are the only vertebrate animals known from Australasia that are restricted to either caves or groundwater.[176] At least 41 terrestrial and 26 aquatic (stygofauna) subterranean species have been discovered in Cape Range[177], including a species of fish, an eel and two species of shrimp: all colourless and blind. Interesting questions are raised as to what they might possibly feed upon.

Cape Range is an elevated limestone plateau dissected by deep gorges and ravines and is interlaced with a network of more than 400 caves. Some scientists argue that Cape Range: "'has the richest and most diverse troglobite [terrestrial animals which are specially adapted to living underground in air-filled, high-humidity caves] community in Australia, and probably the world' and that 'although only very limited investigation has been focused on the area, it has already proven to contain a richness well in excess of that which has been revealed by many decades of detailed investigation elsewhere' including areas where the research effort has been more than 100 times greater than in Cape Range.'"[175]

Shothole Canyon - Cape Range National Park

Shothole Canyon was named after the shot-holes that were created by explosive charges detonated by WAPET in the 1950s while conducting oil seismic surveys. Though oil was found at Rough Range nearby, the well there proved not to be viable and, after many unsuccessful attempts to find oil elsewhere in the region, the WAPET exploration venture was abandoned in 1958.[180]

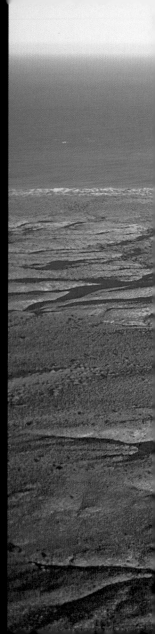

Many of the attributes of these troglobites and stygofauna would appear to have been derived from a time when humid forest is thought to have covered this region. The network of caves, with their high humidity and saline water, have therefore become an important refuge in what is an otherwise dry and stark environment. Similarly, the fact that the stygofauna appear to be unrelated to that of other karst regions of Australia, and share attributes more closely related to those in some islands of the North Atlantic, provides further evidence of continental drift. These stygofauna are believed to have a common origin dating back to the formation of the Tethys Ocean and the concurrent breaking up of the supercontinent, Pangea, into the northern continental mass of Laurasia and the southern mass of Gondwana.[176]

Yardie Creek - Cape Range National Park

Yardie Creek was another photographic challenge. Again, I ventured with a preconceived notion as to how I wanted the photo to look: again, I was frustrated. Initially, I would have loved this shot to show a "glass-off" with the colours of the cliffs being reflected on sundown. However, when I realised that this would not be achievable at sea-level – North-West Cape is susceptible to strong winds at certain times of the year – I took to the air and was rewarded by these magnificent colours. The Indian Ocean can be seen breaking against Ningaloo Reef in the background. "Yardi" appears to be an Aboriginal name meaning creek or river to the Tharrgari/ Payungu tribes.[181]

The Exmouth Gulf Prawn Fishery

Development of the Exmouth Gulf prawn fishery can be traced largely to the efforts of Michael Kailis, founder of the MG Kailis Group. At the time of the fishery's foundation during the early 1960s, Exmouth consisted of little more than a decommissioned airstrip, wheel tracks in the sand and a concrete slab from a fishing base that had been destroyed by a cyclone. Undeterred by the then prevailing view that commercial quantities of prawns did not exist in Exmouth Gulf waters, Kailis persuaded three cray-boat operators to convert their boats to trawlers and commence prawn-fishing operations in the Gulf. At the same time, he established what could only be described as a very basic processing facility. He equipped a shed with a second-hand generator, a mobile freezer that had to be transported 900 kilometres by road at the beginning and end of each season, and an assortment of other items, including a condensor salvaged from a ship-wreck.[182]

Today, the Exmouth Gulf prawn fishery is estimated to turn-over in the vicinity of A$50M annually.[183] Twelve trawlers operate between sunset and sunrise, from April to November, over approximately 200 fishing nights. Of the 1,000 tonnes caught annually, approximately 41% of these are Western King prawns, 35% Brown Tiger prawns and 24% Endeavour prawns. In recent years, the industry has introduced primary and secondary Bi-Catch Reduction Devices ("BRDs") to minimise the size of the non-prawn catch. Primary BRDs mechanically seek to exclude untargeted species according to size and have resulted in their near complete elimination from prawn nets. In broad terms, primary BRDs incorporate a grill at the front of the prawn nets. When the catch is forced toward the rear of the net, larger species hit the grill – they are unable to pass through – and are forced out of the net through a hole in the top. Secondary BRDs separate species by differences in behaviour and are designed to eliminate smaller species not caught by the primary BRD. For example, some fish are capable of swimming in a moving net and are able to escape through an opening in the top of the net. Prawns however display little directional swimming and fall back into the cod-end.[184]

Unloading the Nightly Prawn Catch - The MG Kailis Group - Exmouth

The MG Kailis Group has worked closely with Fisheries to ensure a sustainable prawn operation for the years ahead. Accordingly, the Exmouth Gulf fishery is not a quota-managed area. Instead, Fisheries and operators have focused on maintaining an acceptable catch-range; the objective being to allow stock to mature before it is taken. As soon as the nightly Tiger Prawn catch drops below 19 kilograms per hour, the fishery is closed. Alternatively, if excess breeding stock is found from surveys in November, Fisheries will permit further stock to be taken to ensure that operators maximise their take.[186]

Today, some 40 years after its modest beginnings, the Exmouth Gulf prawn fishery is again being challenged. Ultimately, its ability to withstand this threat will come down to its ability to educate consumers on the shortcomings of the aquaculture product (ie, prawns bred and grown in captivity, both in Australia and overseas). Certainly, I was able to notice the discernable taste difference between the wild and aquaculture product. Exmouth is the only place in Western Australia where prawns are caught and processed daily (its boats come in each morning to unload the night's catch). Wild-caught prawns grow larger than aquaculture-nurtured product as it would simply be too expensive for a prawn farm to wait the length of time required to produce prawns of the size found in the wild. The quality of the Exmouth Gulf water and its nutrients are other factors that distinguish its prawns from aquaculture-grown product. In the latter case, prawns are fed a cocktail of artificial foods designed to optimise growth rate and productivity.[185]

Pulling the Prawn Nets - Exmouth Gulf

Prawns, as a general rule, avoid light (mainly to evade predators: a form of photophobia). However, they are caught more readily in limited light: not complete darkness. The reason for this is not clear. King Prawns tend to live in mud and sand and are the most photophobic of the prawns. Catch productivity tends to fall markedly in the period leading up to, during, and after full moon for this reason. Paradoxically perhaps, the Gulf fished well – particularly for King Prawns - in the period immediately subsequent to Cyclone Vance. Sand and mud stirred up by the cyclone are thought to have given the prawns a false sense of protection and they more readily rose above the seabed. Prawns can also be quite mobile. They move mainly with the tide over distances of up to 20 nautical miles annually.[187]

Ningaloo Marine Park

Extending for a distance of 290 kilometres and located off North-West Cape, Ningaloo Marine Park takes in an area of 4,857 square kilometres.[188] The name "Ningaloo" was taken from nearby Ningaloo Station and approved on 24 November, 1978. It is thought that Ningaloo was once the Aboriginal name for Point Cloates.[189] Ningaloo Marine Park is administered by the Commonwealth and State and was first gazetted by the State as a Marine Park in 1987 and, then, contiguously, by the Commonwealth in 1992. Ningaloo Reef, which falls within the Marine Park, forms a discontinuous barrier that encloses a lagoon. The reef itself is the longest fringing coral reef in Australia: that is, it is located very close to shore. Though the Great Barrier Reef is much longer and incorporates a greater area, it is located much further out to sea than Ningaloo and is not characterised as a fringing reef system. The Ningaloo Reef lagoon varies in width from 200 metres to seven kilometres and retains an average width of 2.5 kilometres.[190]

Ningaloo's flora and fauna species diversity is comparable to that of the Great Barrier Reef at similar latitudes, though its physical structure is less varied. Over 200 species of coral, 600 species of mollusc and 500 species of fish have been discovered within the Park's boundaries: these, in a variety of habitats that include intertidal reef environments, deep oceanic environments off the Continental Shelf, and lagoonal and fringing coral-reef communities.[191]

The Brilliance of the Ningaloo Coastline.

This photograph was taken from a fixed-wing aircraft looking north along the Ningaloo coastline. The mouth of Yardie Creek can be seen in the middle of the frame.

Ningaloo's wide habitat and species diversity is a function of a number of factors. The Continental Shelf off the Cape Range Peninsula is narrower than at any other point in Australia. Deep oceanic waters are therefore closer to the reef and shore. Breaks in the reef allow for regular exchange of water and marine organisms between the deep oceanic waters outside of the reef and the shallow waters between the reef edge and shore. The reef system's unusual proximity to shore is also a function of the region's generally low average rainfall and its low resulting water run-off.[192]

Wildflower Growth - Turquoise Bay.

The Ningaloo beach shots were in some ways the hardest of the book. While the North-West Cape offers some of the most stunning coastal scenery imaginable, the challenge rested on coming up with new angles to vistas that had been photographed many times; this, while still conveying the essence of what it was like to be there. I had first visited the area in late November, 2004 and returned home somewhat disappointed with my results. My return in September, 2005 produced much better results. A different lens and stunning wildflower growth offered life, and a new perspective, to a popular location. The unique water colour at Turquoise Bay is due to a combination of vibrant white sand, crystal-clear water, shallow water depth and illumination by the sun.

each.

September, 2005 visit, to encounter an interesting
around North-West Cape. Typically, skies in the
ded me the opportunity to try angles that might not

Ningaloo Marine Park is a point of convergence for the warmer tropical waters of the north and the cooler temperate waters of the south. The southward flowing Leeuwin Current, which flows most strongly in March and April, brings warm, low-salinity waters and enables tropical species to survive in what would otherwise be temperate conditions. The northerly flowing Ningaloo Current acts as a counter to the Leeuwin Current, and is thought to enable the dispersal of coral larvae following the Autumn mass spawning. It flows most strongly from September to March.[193]

What now remains to be seen is the extent to which Perth-based policy makers are able to balance potentially conflicting objectives. On the one hand there is a desire to facilitate the development of a sustainable eco-tourism industry. On the other, the economic needs of the local recreational fishing industry depend upon the area's fishing grounds for their continued sustenance. Let us hope that the area is managed for the benefit of future generations that live in the area and not only according to the whim of city-centric Government ideologies.

Ningaloo Reef - North-West Cape

According to the former chief geophysicist of the Mundaring Geophysical Observatory (now closed), there have been four recorded major tsunamis on the West Australian coast in the last 20 years. Stemming primarily from undersea earthquakes in the Sunda Arc south of the Indonesian island of Java, it is thought that tsunamis should be expected somewhere along the West Australian coast every 10 to 20 years.

The most recent tsunami to hit Ningaloo occurred on 3 June, 1994. This inundated the beach near Yardie Creek and places further south where the shore was exposed by gaps in the reef. Thousands of fish and crayfish were carried ashore several hundred metres.[194]

Pristine Coastline - Trealla Beach

The Whale Shark (*Rhincodun typus*)[195]

Notwithstanding its many other natural endowments, the area around Exmouth and Ningaloo Reef is perhaps best known for its seasonal Whale Shark population. Each March to June, 200 - 300 immature male Whale Sharks congregate around Ningaloo Reef and its enclosed lagoons. They come to feed on the prolific food chain that exists after the annual mass coral spawning in March and April. Ningaloo is one of the few places around the world where such predictable and reliable aggregation behaviour occurs.

The Whale Shark is a shark, not a whale, and grows to lengths exceeding 12 metres. It is the largest member of the shark family and the largest cold blooded animal on the planet. By contrast, the whale is a mammal (and therefore warm-blooded) and must surface periodically to breath. The largest Whale Shark ever recorded accurately was caught off the coast of India and, at a length of 12.18 metres, weighed in at 11 tonnes. An even larger specimen, claimed to be in excess of 18 metres, was reported in the Gulf of Thailand. However, its size could not be verified and may have been overstated.

Whale Sharks are filter feeders and feed on plankton, small fish and squid. They are found generally between the latitudes of 30 degrees north and 35 degrees south (ie, the warm waters of tropical and sub-tropical seas). They have been found in all major oceans with the exception of the Mediterranean Sea. They have several thousand teeth, arranged in 11 to 12 rows. Each tooth is around two millimetres long and angled back toward the mouth. The teeth are not used during feeding. They feed by filtering small planktonic organisms, up to one millimetre in diameter, through their five gill slits which act like sieves.

The vast majority of Whale Sharks that visit Ningaloo are juvenile males of between three and nine metres in length. Though much remains to be learnt about the animal, preliminary research suggests that the male Whale Shark does not reach sexual maturity until about 30 years of age. If this represents less than one fifth of their life expectancy, this would imply a livespan of over 150 years, making it one of the longest living creatures on the planet. It is thought that the female Whale Shark is ovo-vivi-parous: newborn sharks hatch out of their eggs, inside the body of the mother, before then being expelled. Whale Shark young are thought to range in size from 55 to 63 centimetres.

The Whale Shark - Ningaloo Marine Park

Much remains to be learnt about the Whale Shark. To date, satellite tracking has shown them to dive to depths of up to 700 metres. Little is known about where they breed and how regularly. They have no known predators, with the exception of man. Their liver is huge and is reported to have strong anti-tumour properties. In one 12 metre specimen, the liver was found to weigh one tonne – nine percent of its total body weight.

Notwithstanding assertions that "the first Whale Shark specimen known to science" was discovered off the South African coast in 1828, the 1818 journals of Captain Philip Parker King offer perhaps an even earlier recorded sighting. It notes: "An immense shark was hooked, but it broke the hook and escaped: its length was about twelve feet, of an ashy gray colour, spotted all over with darker marks; the belly was white, and the nose short; it was altogether different from any we had before seen."[196]

©Images of Ningaloo

Coral Bay

The coastline around Coral Bay incorporates some of the wildest and most beautiful coastal dune country that I have encountered. The town of Coral Bay is located at Bills Bay, 234 kilometres to the north of Carnarvon. Perhaps surprisingly, its name was not officially gazetted until 11 January, 2005,[197] though it had been in common usage for many years prior. The town, in turn, appears to have taken its name from the Coral Bay Hotel which was established in 1968 and which, most probably, took its title from the fringing coral reef nearby.[198]

The landing of the schooner, *Maud*, in 1884 at what is now Mauds Landing appears to have been the earliest recorded European activity in the area. Mauds Landing is located some three kilometres to the north of the Coral Bay townsite. In 1896, a *townsite reserve* was gazetted at Mauds Landing to protect the site of an existing jetty and Government storage shed. The jetty incorporated a light rail system to service surrounding pastoralists, both for the dispatch of wool for shipment to Fremantle and for the receipt of supplies. The *name* "Mauds Landing" was officially gazetted in 1915.[199]

Windswept and Windblown – Dune Country – Near Coral Bay.

The town of Coral Bay is located on Bills Bay. Bills Bay was named after Ruby French, a woman who was known by friends as "Auntie Billie". Her husband, Charles French, owned adjacent Cardabia Station. Jack McKenna, the former manager at Mia Mia Station, was the first to build at Bills Bay. He constructed a holiday shack for periodic use during the summer months.[203]

In cases where water depth prevented entry by larger vessels to Mauds Landing, freight was transported to and from the jetty by lighter (a small open cargo boat or barge) through a three-mile-wide opening in the reef nearby.[200] This in itself presented complex challenges. In today's world of telephone, internet and fax interactions, it is easy to overlook the fact that communications around the late 19th Century usually involved telegram. These typically travelled by ship or horse-back. A lighter had to come from Cossack (near Karratha). Not only was it necessary to get the telegram there in time, but arrival of the lighter had to coincide exactly with the arrival of ships to Mauds Landing to avoid delays in their departure.[201] The jetty at Mauds Landing served local pastoralists from 1898 until its closure in 1947.[202]

Sand Contours – Near Coral Bay.

Sand is created through a process of weathering of rock over millennia. The creation of sand from rock and gravel is known as "liberation". Even the sands of the Sahara are the remnants of weathered rock and stone: only 20% of the Sahara is liberated sand. Dunes appear in numerous forms. They are a function of the supply of sand, of which they are made, and the nature of the winds that blow upon them.[204]

Pristine Dune Country – Near Coral Bay.

The Mauds Landing townsite was gazetted into two sections in 1969: a "Northern Section"; and, a "Southern Section". The Northern Section was generally known by the public as Mauds Landing and the Southern Section became known as Coral Bay. In 2004, the Northern Section was abolished and the Southern Section was officially renamed Coral Bay.[205]

A Word from the Photographer about the Equipment Used

There are a number of questions that surface frequently when people ask about the photography that I undertake. Perhaps the most common relates to whether I do my own processing: a question that I answer in the negative. That said, I am finding, as my photographic knowledge deepens, that it is advantageous at the time of making a photograph to know how the different chemicals and emulsions will influence the final outcome. I am hoping, in the years to come, that this is an area in which I can improve significantly. The second relates to the gear that I use. While the camera gear is obviously important, for me, it is the composition, light and quality of film that ultimately separates the "wow" shots from the ordinary. In fact, many of the photos in my first book, and some in this book, were taken with a A$700 Pentax MZ50.

I do not believe in the artificial manipulation of images, whether that be post-processing or by the use of filters (technical correction filters aside). I try to capture a moment in time, as they present to me, using the camera and the film available. That said, film is not a perfect medium and is subject to compromise. It does not replicate colours exactly as they were seen and, Velvia, my film of choice, does have a warming effect on most scenes. Nevertheless, I prefer this approach to what I find the disturbing trend of "playing" with an image so substantially post-processing that it ultimately ends up looking like nothing that was seen when the photographer captured the photograph.

I use a combination of equipment. I have two Canon EOS1N bodies and three lenses: EF 16-35mm f2.8 L USM; EF 50mm f2.5; and, EF 70-200mm f2.8 L IS USM. More recently, I have been shooting with Horseman SW612 Pro equipment due to its bigger transparency size and greater depth of field. Though it can take a variety of backs (eg, 6x7 and 6x9), I use the 612 back exclusively. With it, I use a 55mm lens (equivalent roughly to an 18mm lens in 35mm) and a 135mm lens (roughly equivalent to a 41mm lens in 35mm depending upon the aperture being used).

My limited edition photographic prints are all prepared at the Created for Life Print Studios north of Sydney (02 4365 1488). To my mind, no-one comes close to the quality of prints that they produce: all of which are produced on the finest Ilfochrome archival photographic paper. I use CFL Framing (located north of Sydney) (02 4367 8499) and Gallery 360 in Perth for all of my photographic framing needs (08 9381 6577). The framing of Ilfochrome prints requires special equipment and knowledge that few framers in Australia possess. For my photographic equipment and repair needs, I rely exclusively on Camera Electronics in Perth (08 9328 4405). Their knowledge, reliability and quality of service is truly first-rate.

Photo ©Hazel Blake

Bibliography

Armstrong, J., On the Freedom Track to Narawunda: The Pilbara Aboriginal Pastoral Workers Strike, 1946 – 1998, *Studies in Western Australian History*, 22, 2001, pp. 23-40;

Atherton, G. and Wilkinson, R., *Beyond the Flame: The Story of Australia's North-West Shelf Natural Gas Project*, Griffin Press, Adelaide, Circa 1990;

Barker, H.M., *Camels and the Outback*, Hesperian Press, Perth, 1995;

Battye, J.S., *The History of the North-West of Australia: Embracing Kimberley, Gascoyne and Murchison Districts*, V.K. Jones & Co., Perth, 1915;

Bednarik, R.G., The Survival of the Murujuga (Burrup) Petroglyphs, *Rock Art Research*, Vol.19, No.1, pp.29-40, May 2002, Melbourne;

BHP Iron Ore Pty Ltd, *BHP Iron Ore: World Record Train: 21 June 2001*, BHP Iron Ore Pty Ltd, Perth, 2001;

Burbidge, A.A., *Report VII: Results of a Biological Survey of the Millstream Area*, Department of Fisheries and Fauna, Western Australia, Perth, 1971;

Burdon, A., Karijini Comes of Age, *Australian Geographic: The Journal of the Australian Geographic Society*, Sydney, January – March 1995;

Butler, H., The Canning Stock Route: The Fifth Daniel Brock Memorial Lecture; 1978, Reprinted from the *Proceedings of the Royal Geographical Society of Australasia, South Australian Branch (Inc.), Vol.79, 1978*, Adelaide, 1978;

Butler, H., *Report on an Expedition to the Durba Range: Canning Stock Route, WA*, Unpublished, 28 August, 1971;

Copley, J., Proof of Life, *New Scientist Vol 177 Issue 2383, 22 February 2003*, Reed Business Information Ltd, United Kingdom;

Copp, I., *Geology & Landforms of the Pilbara*, Department of Conservation and Land Management, Perth, 2005;

Cossack Taskforce, *Cossack Conservation and Management Plan: Second Report*, May 1989;

Dames & Moore, *Millstream Water Management Programme*, Engineering Division, Public Works Department, Western Australia, Perth, 1984;

Dampier Port Authority, *History*, Dampier Port Authority, www.dpa.wa.gov.au, 7 October, 2005;

Department of Conservation and Land Management, *Dampier Archipelago Nature Reserves: Management Plan 1990 – 2000*, CALM, Perth, 1989;

Department of Conservation and Land Management, *Karijini National Park: Management Plan 1999 – 2009*, CALM, Perth, 1999;

Department of Conservation and Land Management, *Naturebase*, Park of the Month, Millstream-Chichester National Park, Internet, Perth, June 1997;

Department of Conservation and Land Management, *Naturebase*, Park of the Month, Rudall River National Park, Internet, Perth, May, 1999;

Department of Conservation and Land Management, *Ningaloo Marine Park Draft Management Plan and Indicative Management Plans for the Extension to the Existing Park and the Proposed Muiron Islands Marine Management Area*, CALM, Perth, 2004;

Department of Conservation and Land Management, *Nomenclature of Proposed National Park, Hamersley Ranges*, CALM, Perth, Circa 1960s;

Department of Mineral and Petroleum Resources, *Western Australia: Iron Ore Industry: September 2002*, Department of Mineral and Petroleum Resources, Perth, 2002;

Department of Resources Development, Communications Branch, *Karratha*, June 1994;

Donaldson, M., and Elliot, I., *Do Not Yield to Despair: Frank Hugh Hann's Exploration Diaries in the Arid Interior of Australia: 1895-1908*, Hesperian Press, Perth, 1998;

Duckett, B., *Red Dog: The Pilbara Wanderer*, Duckett, B., 1993;

Edmondson, M., *Reflections: 20 Years of Robe*, Robe River Iron Associates, 1992;

Edwards, H., *Gold Dust & Iron Mountains: Marble Bar and Beyond*, Hugh Edwards, Swanbourne, 1993;

Environmental Protection Authority, *Environmental Protection of Cape Range Province: Position Statement No.1*, Environmental Protection Authority, Perth, December 1999;

Evans, W., Dam Fills to Capacity, *The West Australian*, Thursday, March 4, 1982, Perth, 1982;

Evans, W., Ophthalmia Dam Nears Completion, *News of the North*, 12 November 1981, Perth, 1981;

Evans, W., Water Supply Breaks New Ground, *News of the North*, Publication Date not Known;

Giles, E., *Australia Twice Traversed*, Hesperian Press, Perth, 1995;

Gregory, A.C., and Gregory, F.T., *Journals of Australian Explorations 1846 – 1861*, Hesperian Press, Perth, 2002;

Hamersley Iron Pty Ltd, *Hamersley Iron Fact Sheet: Dampier Port*, Hamersley Iron Pty Ltd, Internet, Date Unknown;

Hamersley Iron Pty Ltd, *Technical Fact book 2003*, Hamersley Iron Pty Ltd, (www.pilbarairon.com), 2003;

Hamersley News, Karratha – Town of Rapid Progress, *Hamersley News*, Thursday, November 22, 1973;

Hardie, J., *Nor'Westers of the Pilbara Breed: The Story of the Brave Ancestors who Pioneered the Outback Pilbara in Western Australia*, Hesperian Press, Perth, 2001;

Heritage Council of Western Australia, *Emma Withnell Heritage Trail: Settlement and Development of the Roebourne District*, Heritage Council of Western Australia, Perth, Circa 1990;

De Havelland, D.W., *Gold and Ghosts*, Hesperian Press, Perth, 1985;

Jarvis, T., Adventure vs Exploration, *The Bulletin*, December 21, 2004 – January 11, 2005, ACP Publishing Pty Ltd, Sydney, 2004;

King, Captain Philip Parker, *Narrative of a Survey of the Intertropical and Western Coast of Australia, performed between the years 1818 and 1821*, Two Volumes, John Murray, London, 1827;

Lynch, J., *Wild Weather*, BBC Worldwide Limited, London, 2002;

Macrae, B., *Hills Been Travelling: A Story of the Pilbara*, Public Relations Group, Robe River Iron Associates, Wickham, 1991;

McDonald, R., *Along the Ashburton*, Hesperian Press, Perth, 2002;

McIllraith, J., *The First 500 Million: The Mt Newman Story*, Public Affairs Department, Iron Ore BHP-Utah Minerals International, Perth, 1988;

McIllwraith, J., *Title Unknown*, Robe River Iron Associates, Wickham, 1997;

MG Kailis Group, *MG Kailis Exmouth Prawns: Pioneers of the Exmouth Gulf*, MG Kailis Group, Perth, Circa 2004;

Morton, S.R., Short, S., and Barker, R.D., *Refugia for Biological Diversity in Arid and Semi-Arid Australia, Biodiversity Series*, Paper No.4, Biodiversity Unit, Department of the Environment and Heritage, Internet, 2004;

Muir, P., *Blue Peaks and Red Ridges: the 1965-66 Campfire Field Notes of Desert Explorations in WA*, Western Desert Guides Publishing, Perth, 1996;

Murdoch University, The Natural Environment Documentation Project, *Eighty-Mile Beach Area: Supporting Documentation for Inclusion on the Register of the National Estate*, The Natural Environment Documentation Project, Murdoch University, Perth, 1993;

Murray, R., *From the Edge of a Timeless Land*, Allen & Unwin Pty Ltd, Sydney, 1991;

Newman's New Dam Results in Clearer Tap Water, *Newman Chronicle*, June, 1982;

Normalisation – A Most Satisfactory First Year, *Newman Chronicle*, Circa 1982;

O'Brien Planning Consultants, *Thematic Framework for the Shire of Exmouth Municipal Heritage Inventory*, Shire of Exmouth, Perth, January, 1998;

Oklahoma State University Board of Regents, *Breeds of Livestock: Brahman*, Internet, 2000;

Panizza, J., *The Discovery of Gold and the Development of the Nullagine District 1886 to 1906*, Lee Steer Competition, Western Australian Historical Society, Unpublished, 1966;

Pannawonica Occasional Child Care Centre, *Pannawonica Telephone Directory*, Pannawonica Occasional Child Care Centre, 2005;

Port Hedland Port Authority, *2004/2005 Cargo Statistics and Port Information*, Port Hedland Port Authority, Port Hedland, 2005;

Porter GeoConsultancy Pty Ltd, *World Ore Deposit Database: Mt Whaleback*, Internet, Linden Park, South Australia, 2002;

Rinehart, G., *50 Year Historic Commemoration Speech: 22 November 2002*, Hancock Prospecting, (www.hancockprospecting.com.au), 2002;

Robe River Iron Associates, *Corporate Profile Factsheet*, Robe River Iron Associates, (Publication Date Unknown);

Rudall, W.F., *Field Book 6*, Unpublished, (Date Unknown);

Sharp, E.I., *Some Ghosts, Some Not*, Sharp, E.I., 1979;

Smith, M., *A Summary of the Geology of the Karijini National Park*, Geological Survey of Western Australia, Unpublished, 1998;

Taylor, G., *Whale Sharks: The Giants of Ningaloo Reef*, Angus & Robertson, 1994;

Terry, M., The Canning Basin of Western Australia, *Geographical Journal*: Vol. 123, No.2, pp. 157 – 166 (Publication Date not Known);

Tropical Savannas CRC, Termites, *Tropical Topics: An Interpretative Newsletter for the Tourism Industry*, No.64, December, 2000,

University of Western Australia, *Media Statement*, University of Western Australia, Internet, August 1998;

Van Kranendonk, M.J., Hickman, A.U., Smithies, R.H., Nelson, D.R. and Pike, G., Geology and Tectonic Evolution of the Archean North Pilbara Terrain, Pilbara Craton, Western Australia, *Economic Geology*, Vol.97. 2002, at p.703;

Veth, P., Bradshaw, E., Gara, T., Hall, N., Haydock, P., and Kendrick, P., *Burrup Peninsula Aboriginal Heritage Project: A Report to the Department of Conservation and Land Management*, 1993;

Vinnicombe, R.G., Petroglyphs of the Dampier Archipelago; Background to Development and Descriptive Analysis, *Rock Art Research*, Vol.19, No.1, May 2002, Melbourne at pp.3-27;

Vitenbergs, A. and Brehaut, L., *Pilbara Journey Through the Twentieth Century: From Transcripts Collected by Anna Vitenbergs & Loreen Brehaut: Edited by Trevor Douglass*, Robe River Iron Associates, Perth, 2000;

Webb, M. and A., *Robe's 20 Years*, Artlook Books, Perth, 1983;

Whelan, H., Where Deserts Meet: Rudall River National Park, *Australian Geographic: The Journal of the Australian Geographic Society*, Sydney, October – December, 1997 at pp. 92-117;

Wittenoom Progress Association, *Wittenoom: Central to the Karijini Gorges*, Wittenoom Progress Association, Perth, 2004; and,

Woldendorp, R., and McIllwraith, J., *Hamersley Iron: Twenty Five Years*, Hamersley Iron Pty Ltd, Perth, 1991.

Footnotes

1 Jarvis, T., Adventure vs Exploration, *The Bulletin*, December 21, 2004 – January 11, 2005, ACP, Publishing Pty Ltd, Sydney, 2004;

2 Muir, P., *Blue Peaks and Red Ridges: the 1965-66 Campfire Field Notes of Desert Explorations in W A*, WDG Publishing, Perth 1996 at p.359;

3 HF is short for High Frequency. Radios of this type are used for communications extending from distances of several hundred kilometres to several thousand kilometres.

4 UHF is short for Ultra High Frequency. Radios of this type are typically used for short distance communications: usually, line of sight.

5 Hardie, J., *Nor'Westers of the Pilbara Breed: The Story of the Brave Ancestors who Pioneered the Outback Pilbara in Western Australia*, Hesperian Press, Perth, 2001;

6 Ibid;

7 Ibid;

8 Port Hedland Port Authority, *2004/2005 Cargo Statistics and Port Information*, Port Hedland Port Authority, Port Hedland, 2005;

9 Information gained from personal verbal communications with BHP staff and suppliers;

10 Ibid;

11 Ibid;

12 Information gleaned from personal verbal communications with onsite geologists;

13 This information was obtained in verbal personal communications with Denis O'Meara;

14 This information was obtained during verbal personal communications with a geologist working in the area of DOM's Hill;

15 Murdoch University, The Natural Environment Documentation Project, *Eighty-Mile Beach Area: Supporting Documentation for Inclusion on the Register of the National Estate*, The Natural Environment Documentation Project, Murdoch University, Perth, 1993;

16 For much of this information, I am indebted to Brian Goodchild, Secretary of the Geographic Names Committee at the Department of Land Information. This was obtained through personal email correspondence with Mr Goodchild.

17 See Van Kranendonk, M.J., Hickman, A.U., Smithies, R.H., Nelson, D.R. and Pike, G., Geology and Tectonic Evolution of the Archean North Pilbara Terrain, Pilbara Craton, Western Australia, *Economic Geology*, Vol.97. 2002 at p.703

18 An excellent discussion of the link between stromatolites and the beginnings of life on earth is contained in Copley, J., Proof of Life, *New Scientist Vol 177 Issue 2383, 22 February 2003*, Reed Business Information Ltd, United Kingdom, 2003. Just under 99% of all earthly carbon exists as the stable carbon-12 isotope with the remainder existing as carbon-13. Living organisms and fossils have higher proportions of carbon-12 than does inorganic matter. Proponents of the stromatolite school of thought point to the fact that the ratio of carbon-12 to carbon-13 tallies with the ratios that would be expected with early life. Those against the theory argue that complex and sophisticated stromatolites can be created via means other than life (eg, around volcanic springs on the sea floor) and that the stromatolite beds around Marble Bar were the upper part of a dyke or volcanic pipe. If this argument is accurate serious questions are raised as to whether photosynthetic bacteria could survive up to two kilometres into the earth's crust.

19 Edwards, H., *Gold Dust & Iron Mountains: Marble Bar and Beyond*, Hugh Edwards, Swanbourne, 1993 at pp 172-177;

20 For the content of this text, I am indebted to Martin Van Kranendonk at the Western Australian Geological Survey and to whom I owe a big thank you!

21 Lynch, J., *Wild Weather*, BBC Worldwide Limited, London, 2002 at pp.190-191;

22 Based on an analysis of data sets supplied by the Bureau of Meteorology. For this, I must direct a great thank you to Brian and the "Weather Ferret" who provided fantastic assistance.

23 Geographic Place Names, Department of Land Information;

24 Gregory, A.C., and Gregory, F.T., *Journals of Australian Explorations 1846 – 1861*, Hesperian Press, Perth, 2002 at pp.77-8;

25 Gregory, A.C., and Gregory, F.T., *Journals of Australian Explorations 1846 – 1861*, Hesperian Press, Perth, 2002 at p.79;

26 Based on anecdotal information provided in personal verbal communications with Alex Dorrington, a long-time Marble Bar resident;

27 Hardie, J., *Nor'Westers of the Pilbara Breed: The Story of the Brave Ancestors who Pioneered the Outback Pilbara in Western Australia*, Hesperian Press, Perth, 2001 at pp. 175-188;

28 Armstrong, J., On the Freedom Track to Narawunda: The Pilbara Aboriginal Pastoral Workers Strike, 1946 – 1998, *Studies in Western Australian History*, 22, 2001, pp. 23-40;

29 Barker, H.M., *Camels and the Outback*, Hesperian Press, Perth, 1995 at p.173;

30 Aboriginal groups tend to refer to different parts of a river with different names and do not typically accord a single name to any one river.

31 Donaldson, M., and Elliot, I., *Do Not Yield to Despair: Frank Hugh Hann's Exploration Diaries in the Arid Interior of Australia: 1895-1908*, Hesperian Press, Perth, 1998 at pp.31-2;

32 Department of Conservation and Land Management, *Naturebase*, Park of the Month, Rudall River National Park, Internet, Perth, May, 1999;

33 Whelan, H. Where Deserts Meet: Rudall River National Park, *Australian Geographic: The Journal of the Australian Geographic Society*, Sydney, October – December 1997 at p.104;

34 Ibid at p.96;

35 Ibid at p.99;

36 Ibid at p.107;

37 University of Western Australia, *Media Statement*, University of Western Australia, Internet, August 1998;

38 Whelan, H. Where Deserts Meet: Rudall River National Park, *Australian Geographic: The Journal of the Australian Geographic Society*, Sydney, October – December 1997 at p.114;

39 Barker, H.M., *Camels and the Outback*, Hesperian Press, Perth, 1995;

40 Department of Land Information;

41 Whelan, H., Where Deserts Meet: Rudall River National Park, *Australian Geographic: The Journal of the Australian Geographic Society*, Sydney, October – December 1997 at p.98;

42 Rudall, W.F., *Field Book 6*, Unpublished at pp.72-3;

43 Donaldson, M., and Elliot, I., *Do Not Yield to Despair: Frank Hugh Hann's Exploration Diaries in the Arid Interior of Australia: 1895-1908*, Hesperian Press, Perth, 1998 at p.36;

44 Butler, H., The Canning Stock Route: The Fifth Daniel Brock Memorial Lecture; 1978, Reprinted from the *Proceedings of the Royal Geographical Society of Australasia, South Australian Branch (Inc.), Vol.79, 1978*, Adelaide, 1978;

45 Terry, M., The Canning Basin of Western Australia, *Geographical Journal: Vol. 123, No.2* at p.159;

46 Most of the information in the text here was obtained from the following source: Panizza, J., *The Discovery of Gold and the Development of the Nullagine District 1886 to 1906*, Lee Steer Competition, Western Australian Historical Society, Unpublished, 1966;

47 McIllraith, J., *The First 500 Million: The Mt Newman Story*, Public Affairs Department, Iron Ore BHP-Utah Minerals International, Perth, 1988 at p.14;

48 Porter GeoConsultancy Pty Ltd, *World Ore Deposit Database: Mt Whaleback*, Internet, Linden Park, South Australia, 2002;

49 This information was obtained from personal verbal communications with a Mt Whaleback contractor;

50 McIllraith, J., *The First 500 Million: The Mt Newman Story*, Public Affairs Department, Iron Ore BHP-Utah Minerals International, Perth, 1988 at pp.25 & 35;

51 Ibid at p.19;

52 *Mt Newman Chronicle*, Normalisation – A Most Satisfactory First Year, Newman, Circa 1982 (page number not known);

53 McIllraith, J., *The First 500 Million: The Mt Newman Story*, Public Affairs Department, Iron Ore BHP-Utah Minerals International, Perth, 1988 at p.18;

54 Gregory, A.C., and Gregory, F.T., *Journals of Australian Explorations 1846 – 1861*, Hesperian Press, Perth, 2002 at p.78;

55 Information taken from personal verbal communications with Denis and Damon O'Meara: proprietors of Outback Trees of Australia. Outback Trees undertake mine-site rehabilitation throughout Australia using local native vegetation;

56 Geographic Names, Department of Land Information;

57 Sourced from discussions with members of the local Nyiyaparli and Martu Aboriginal peoples;

58 Gregory, A.C., and Gregory, F.T., *Journals of Australian Explorations 1846 – 1861*, Hesperian Press, Perth, 2002 at p.60;

59 Lynch, J., *Wild Weather*, BBC Worldwide Limited, London, 2002. An excellent lay discussion of the processes giving rise to thunder and lightning, and the weather more generally is contained in this very readable, interesting and enjoyable book;

60 Giles, E., *Australia Twice Traversed*, Hesperian Press, Perth, 1995;

61 Gregory, A.C., and Gregory, F.T., *Journals of Australian Explorations 1846 – 1861*, Hesperian Press, Perth, 2002 at p.62;

62 Ibid;

63 Gregory, A.C., and Gregory, F.T., *Journals of Australian Explorations 1846 – 1861*, Hesperian Press, Perth, 2002 at p.69;

64 Smith, M., *A Summary of the Geology of the Karijini National Park*, Geological Survey of Western Australia, Unpublished, 1998. I am also indebted to Martin van Kranendonk for his invaluable assistance in helping me to understand the geology of the Hamersley and Chichester Ranges and Ashburton Basin;

65 Ibid;

66 Ibid;

67 Based on verbal personal communications with Sean O'Connor, a geophysicist undertaking contract work for a mining company in the region;

68 Geographic Names, Department of Land Information;

69 Department of Conservation and Land Management, *Nomenclature of Proposed National Park, Hamersley Ranges*, CALM, Perth, C 1960s;

70 Ibid;

71 Smith, M., *A Summary of the Geology of the Karijini National Park*, Geological Survey of Western Australia, Unpublished, 1998;

72 Department of Conservation and Land Management, *Nomenclature of Proposed National Park, Hamersley Ranges*, CALM, Perth, C 1960s;

73 Geographic Names, Department of Land Information;

74 Department of Conservation and Land Management, *Nomenclature of Proposed National Park, Hamersley Ranges*, CALM, Perth, C 1960s;

75 This information is based on personal email communications with Dr Martin van Kranendonk of the Geological Survey of Western Australia;

76 Ibid;

77 Dept. of Conservation and Land Management, *Karijini National Park: Management Plan 1999 – 2009*, CALM, Perth, 1999 at pp.22 - 28;

78 Ibid at p.27;

79 Edmondson, M., *Reflections: 20 Years of Robe*, Robe River Iron Associates, 1992 at p.2;

80 Edwards, H., *Gold Dust & Iron Mountains: Marble Bar and Beyond*, Hugh Edwards, Swanbourne, 1993 at p.231;

81 Rinehart, G.,50 Year Historic Commemoration Speech: 22 November 2002, Hancock Prospecting, Internet, 2002;

82 Ibid;

83 Edwards, H., *Gold Dust & Iron Mountains: Marble Bar and Beyond*, Hugh Edwards, Swanbourne, 1993 at p.233;

84 Ibid at p.234;

85 Ibid at p.232;

86 BHP Iron Ore Pty Ltd, *BHP Iron Ore: World Record Train: 21 June 2001*, BHP Iron Ore Pty Ltd, Perth, 2001;

87 Geographic Names, Department of Land Information;

88 Information here gained from correspondence with Pilbara Iron Public Affairs;

89 Hamersley Iron Pty Ltd, *Technical Fact Book 2003*, Hamersley Iron Pty Ltd, Internet, 2003;

90 This information was taken from a newspaper clipping held by the Paraburdoo Public Library. The article is entitled "Theories on name's origin" but no author or newspaper title was attributed;

91 Geographic Names, Department of Land Information;

92 Ibid;

93 Dept. of Conservation and Land Management, *Karijini National Park: Management Plan 1999 – 2009*, CALM, Perth, 1999 at p.23;

94 Information here obtained from Dr Martin van Kranendonk of the Geological Survey of Western Australia;

95 Edmondson, M., *Reflections: 20 Years of Robe*, Robe River Iron Associates, 1992 at p.5;

96 Geographic Names, Department of Land Information;

97 Edmondson, M., *Reflections: 20 Years of Robe*, Robe River Iron Associates, 1992 at p.2;

98 This information was gleaned from the following source: Macrae, B., *Hills Been Travelling: A Story of the Pilbara*, Public Relations Group, Robe River Iron Associates, Wickham, 1991;

99 Webb, M. and A., *Robe's 20 Years*, Artlook Books, Perth, 1983;

100 Information gleaned from verbal interviews with Mesa J mine staff; on 12 August, 2005;

101 Edmondson, M., *Reflections: 20 Years of Robe*, Robe River Iron Associates, 1992 at p.2;

102 Geographic Names, Department of Land Information;

103 Pannawonica Occasional Child Care Centre, *Pannawonica Telephone Directory*, Pannawonica Occasional Child Care Centre, 2005;

104 De Havelland, D.W., *Gold and Ghosts*, Hesperian Press, Perth, 1985 at pp.47-50;

105 Geographic Names, Department of Land Information;

106 Gregory, A.C., and Gregory, F.T., *Journals of Australian Explorations 1846 – 1861*, Hesperian Press, Perth, 2002 at p.63;

107 Ibid;

108 Department of Conservation and Land Management, *Naturebase*, Park of the Month, Millstream-Chichester National Park, Perth, June 1007;

109 Dames & Moore, *Millstream Water Management Programme*, Engineering Division, Public Works Department, Western Australia, Perth, 1984 at p.19;

110 Burbidge, A.A., *Report VII: Results of a Biological Survey of the Millstream Area*, Department of Fisheries and Fauna, Western Australia, Perth, 1971;

111 Dames & Moore, *Millstream Water Management Programme*, Engineering Division, Public Works Department, Western Australia, Perth, 1984 at p.64;

112 Gregory, A.C., and Gregory, F.T., *Journals of Australian Explorations 1846 – 1861*, Hesperian Press, Perth, 2002 at p.61;

113 Burbidge, A.A., *Report VII: Results of a Biological Survey of the Millstream Area*, Department of Fisheries and Fauna, Western Australia, Perth, 1971;

114 Dames & Moore, *Millstream Water Management Programme*, Engineering Division, Public Works Department, Western Australia, Perth, 1984;

115 Geographic Names, Department of Land Information;

116 Gregory, A.C., and Gregory, F.T., *Journals of Australian Explorations 1846 – 1861*, Hesperian Press, Perth, 2002 at p.62;

117 Copp, I., *Geology & Landforms of the Pilbara*, Department of Conservation and Land Management, Perth, 2005 at P.26;

118 Wittenoom Progress Association, *Wittenoom: Central to the Karijini Gorges*, Wittenoom Progress Association, Perth, 2004;

119 Geographic Names, Department of Land Information;

120 Wittenoom Progress Association, *Wittenoom: Central to the Karijini Gorges*, Wittenoom Progress Association, Perth, 2004;

121 Ibid;

122 In 1986, the Environment Protection Authority undertook a study into airborne asbestos levels at Wittenoom townsite (See Dept. of Conservation and Land Management, *Karijini National Park: Management Plan 1999 – 2009*, CALM, Perth, 1999). It did not establish a correlation between airborne asbestos levels and wind direction and/or speed. This suggests, perhaps, that the fact that it did not establish a correlation does not rule out the possibility that one exists. That study was undertaken when winds were blowing from the north-west and would appear not to have been undertaken during the winter months when easterly winds tend to dominate;

123 Information obtained from personal verbal communication with town residents on 28 September, 2005;

124 The majority of the Roebourne information was sourced from the following reference: Heritage Council of Western Australia, *Emma Withnell Heritage Trail: Settlement and Development of the Roebourne District*, Heritage Council of Western Australia, Perth, Circa 1990;

125 The first settler, of European descent, in the district was Walter Padbury, who arrived in the area in 1863;

126 Mt Welcome was known to the Aborigines as Yeera-muk-a-doo which refers to a wild fig which grew in profusion in the area;

127 Geographic Names, Department of Land Information;

128 Cossack Taskforce, *Cossack Conservation and Management Plan: Second Report*, May 1989;

129 Ibid;

130 Ibid;

131 Cossack Taskforce, *Cossack Conservation and Management Plan: Second Report*, May 1989 at p.4;

132 Geographic Names, Department of Land Information;

133 McIllwraith,J., *Title Unknown*, Robe River Iron Associates, Wickham, 1997 at pp. 26 – 30;

134 Robe River Iron Associates, *Corporate Profile Factsheet*, Robe River Iron Associates at p.7;

135 This information was sourced from the Pilbara Iron website (www.pilbarairon.com) on 5 October 2005;

136 Heritage Council of Western Australia, *Emma Withnell Heritage Trail: Settlement and Development of the Roebourne District*, Heritage Council of Western Australia, Perth, Circa 1990;

137 Geographic Names, Department of Land Information;

138 Geographic Names, Department of Land Information;

139 Hamersley News, Karratha – Town of Rapid Progress, *Hamersley News*, Thursday, November 22, 1973;

140 Estimate based on 1996 Census finding of 10,057 and projected average annual compound population growth since that time of 5%;

141 Murray, R., *From the Edge of a Timeless Land*, Allen & Unwin Pty Ltd, Sydney, 1991 at p.188;

142 King, Captain Philip Parker, *Narrative of a Survey of the Intertropical and Western Coast of Australia, performed between the years 1818 and 1821*, Two Volumes, John Murray, London, 1827 at p.52;

143 Geographic Names, Department of Land Information;

144 Woldendorp, R., and McIllwraith, J., *Hamersley Iron: Twenty Five Years*, Hamersley Iron Pty Ltd, Perth, 1991 at pp. 8 – 29;

145 Dampier Port Authority, *History*, Dampier Port Authority, Internet, September, 2005;

146 Dampier Port Authority, *Cargo Statistics*, Dampier Port Authority, Internet, September, 2005;

147 Duckett, B., *Red Dog: The Pilbara Wanderer*, Duckett, B., 1993;

148 Dampier Port Authority, *History*, Dampier Port Authority, Internet, September, 2005;

149 Woldendorp, R., and McIllwraith, J., *Hamersley Iron: Twenty Five Years*, Hamersley Iron Pty Ltd, Perth, 1991 at pp. 8 – 29;

150 Based on personal verbal communications with the Dampier Harbour Master;

151 The material for this text was drawn from the following publication: Atherton, G. and Wilkinson, R., *Beyond the Flame: The Story of Australia's North-West Shelf Natural Gas Project*, Griffin Press, Adelaide, Circa 1990;

152 Information sourced from Woodside website (www.woodside.com.au) on 6 October, 2005;

153 Bednarik, R.G., The Survival of the Murujuga (Burrup) Petroglyphs, *Rock Art Research*, Vol.19, No.1, May 2002, Melbourne at p.29;

154 Vinnicombe, R.G., Petroglyphs of the Dampier Archipelago; Background to Development and Descriptive Analysis, *Rock Art Research*, Vol.19, No.1, May 2002, Melbourne at p.23;

155 Veth, P., Bradshaw, E., Gara, T., Hall, N., Haydock, P., and Kendrick, P., *Burrup Peninsula Aboriginal Heritage Project: A Report to the Department of Conservation and Land Management*, 1993 at p.73;

156 Vinnicombe, R.G., Petroglyphs of the Dampier Archipelago; Background to Development and Descriptive Analysis, *Rock Art Research*, Vol.19, No.1, May 2002, Melbourne at pp.22-23;

157 Veth, P., Bradshaw, E., Gara, T., Hall, N., Haydock, P., and Kendrick, P., *Burrup Peninsula Aboriginal Heritage Project: A Report to the Department of Conservation and Land Management*, 1993 at pp.49-59;

158 Copp, I., *Geology & Landforms of the Pilbara*, Department of Conservation and Land Management, Perth, 2005 at p.20;

159 Ibid;

160 Gregory, A.C., and Gregory, F.T., *Journals of Australian Explorations 1846 – 1861*, Hesperian Press, Perth, 2002 at p.57;

161 Veth, P., Bradshaw, E., Gara, T., Hall, N., Haydock, P., and Kendrick, P., *Burrup Peninsula Aboriginal Heritage Project: A Report to the Department of Conservation and Land Management*, 1993 at p.226;

162 Information for this text was sourced from the following reference: Department of Conservation and Land Management, *Dampier Archipelago Nature Reserves: Management Plan 1990 – 2000*, CALM, Perth, 1989;

163 The information for this text was drawn from the following source: McDonald, R., *Along the Ashburton*, Hesperian Press, Perth, 2002;

164 Tropical Savannas CRC, Termites, *Tropical Topics: An Interpretative Newsletter for the Tourism Industry*, No. 64, December 2000;

165 The above statistics are estimates only and were obtained in personal verbal communications from the Department of Agriculture on 23 September, 2005. Reliable numbers are hard to obtain due to the fact that virtually all of the herd turn-off goes through Midland in Perth and there is no requirement for pastoralists to provide turn-off numbers;

166 Oklahoma State University Board of Regents, *Breeds of Livestock: Brahman*, Internet, 2000;

167 O'Brien Planning Consultants, *Thematic Framework for the Shire of Exmouth Municipal Heritage Inventory*, Shire of Exmouth, Perth, January 1998;

168 Ibid;

169 King, Captain Philip Parker, *Narrative of a Survey of the Intertropical and Western Coast of Australia, performed between the years 1818 and 1821*, Two Volumes, John Murray, London, 1827 at p.29;

170 Ibid;

171 Ibid at p.21;

172 Environmental Protection Authority, *Environmental Protection of Cape Range Province: Position Statement No.1*, Environmental Protection Authority, Perth, December 1999 at p.6;

173 Ibid at p.4;

174 Ibid;

175 Ibid at pp.6-7;

176 Ibid;

177 Morton, S.R., Short, S., and Barker, R.D., *Refugia for Biological Diversity in Arid and Semi-Arid Australia, Biodiversity Series*, Paper No.4, Biodiversity Unit, Department of the Environment and Heritage, Internet, 2004 at p.3;

178 Environmental Protection Authority, *Environmental Protection of Cape Range Province: Position Statement No.1*, Environmental Protection Authority, Perth, December 1999; at pp. 6-7;

179 O'Brien Planning Consultants, *Thematic Framework for the Shire of Exmouth Municipal Heritage Inventory*, Shire of Exmouth, Perth, January 1998 at Place No.4/ Charles Knife Road/ Page 2;

180 Ibid at page 8 and Place No. 12/ Shothole Canyon and Road/ Page 2;

181 Geographic Names, Department of Land Information;

182 MG Kailis Group, *MG Kailis Exmouth Prawns: Pioneers of the Exmouth Gulf*, MG Kailis Group, Perth, Circa 2004;

183 Based on personal verbal communications with a Department of Fisheries officer on 16 and 17 September, 2005;

184 Department of Fisheries information wall-chart;

185 Based on personal verbal communications with Industry sources;

186 Based on personal verbal communications with MG Kailis staff and a Department of Fisheries officer on 16 and 17 September, 2005;

187 Ibid;

188 Environment Australia, *Ningaloo Marine Park (Commonwealth Waters): Management Plan 2002*, Environment Australia, Canberra, 2002 at p.17;

189 Geographic Names, Department of Land Information;

190 Department of Conservation and Land Management, *Ningaloo Marine Park Draft Management Plan and Indicative Management Plans for the Extension to the Existing Park and the Proposed Muiron Islands Marine Management Area*, CALM, Perth, 2004 at p.9;

191 Ibid at p.11;

192 Ibid at p.9;

193 Environment Australia, *Ningaloo Marine Park (Commonwealth Waters): Management Plan 2002*, Environment Australia, Canberra, 2002 at pp. 18-19;

194 Environment Australia, *Ningaloo Marine Park (Commonwealth Waters): Management Plan 2002*, Environment Australia, Canberra, 2002 at p.22;

195 The majority of the information drawn for this section was drawn from the excellent publication by Geoff Taylor. Its citation is as follows: Taylor, G., *Whale Sharks: The Giants of Ningaloo Reef*, Angus & Robertson, 1994;

196 King, Captain Philip Parker, *Narrative of a Survey of the Intertropical and Western Coast of Australia, performed between the years 1818 and 1821*, Two Volumes, John Murray, London, 1827 at p.27;

197 Geographic Names, Department of Land Information;

198 Information here taken from www.coralbay.info on 7 October, 2005;

199 Ibid;

200 Information obtained here on 7 October, 2005, from personal verbal communications with former long-time resident, Rick French;

201 Ibid;

202 Information here taken from www.coralbay.info on 7 October, 2005;

203 Ibid;

204 Lynch, J., *Wild Weather*, BBC Worldwide Limited, London, 2002 at pp.183-5;

205 Geographic Names, Department of Land Information;